UNCOMMON

UNCOMMON

SIMPLE PRINCIPLES
for an
EXTRAORDINARY LIFE

Mark Divine

**ST. MARTIN'S
PRESS
NEW YORK**

First published in the United States by St. Martin's Press, an imprint of St. Martin's Publishing Group

www.stmartins.com

Designed by Steven Seighman

Library of Congress Cataloging-in-Publication Data

Names: Divine, Mark, author.
Title: Uncommon : simple principles for an extraordinary life / Mark Divine.
Description: First edition. | New York : St. Martin's Press, 2024. | Includes bibliographical references.
Identifiers: LCCN 2023058077 | ISBN 9781250331908 (hardcover) | ISBN 9781250331915 (ebook)
Subjects: LCSH: Businesspeople—United States—Biography. | Leaders—United States—Biography. | United States. Navy. SEALs—Biography. | Motivation (Psychology) | Conduct of life.
Classification: LCC HC102.5.A3 D585 2024 | DDC 650.1—dc23/eng/20240131
LC record available at https://lccn.loc.gov/2023058077

Our books may be purchased in bulk for promotional, educational, or business use. Please contact your local bookseller or the Macmillan Corporate and Premium Sales Department at 1-800-221-7945, extension 5442, or by email at MacmillanSpecialMarkets@macmillan.com.

First Edition: 2024

10 9 8 7 6 5 4 3 2 1

CONTENTS

INTRODUCTION

COMMON is going to business school because Dad approves, though your dream is to be a Navy SEAL or become a digital nomad.

COMMON is continuing to eat crappy food because you don't have the time to prepare healthy meals.

COMMON is knowing your relationship isn't going to last but not having the courage to end it.

COMMON is blowing off studying for the kegger—you'll make up the studying the next day.

COMMON is blaming your parents for your less savory qualities, rather than taking control of your mind and life to change things for the better.

COMMON is dreaming about becoming an über-successful entrepreneur during your nine-to-five, yet not taking definitive, daily action toward the goal.

COMMON is keeping your mouth shut when you see abuse or injustice because you're afraid to take any action.

COMMON is knowing there's an entrepreneur, warrior, artist, teacher, or influencer inside you, but you're too paralyzed by imposter syndrome to pursue it.

DON'T LET THIS BE YOU.

If any of the above statements define you in some way, then it's time to take charge of, and commit to, a new way.

I'm Mark Divine. If you're familiar with my mission, thank you for joining me on yet another journey. If we're just meeting, here's the lowdown: I'm a college athlete turned CPA who ditched corporate America to become an elite Navy SEAL, then entrepreneur, author, speaker, professor of leadership, and philanthropist. I'm the creator of SEAL-FIT, Kokoro Yoga, and Unbeatable Mind, and I've written six books, including *New York Times, Wall Street Journal,* and Amazon bestsellers.

I look really good on paper, right? So what.

Here's the million-dollar question: *What makes me qualified to teach you?*

Let me start by telling you that it's not my credentials. Though you might view them as uncommon, they're just outward signs that I can think relatively well. The real reason I can guide you to your Uncommon Life is because I ripped each one of the opening statements from the pages of my own life. The reason *I'm the guy* is because I used to be common myself.

In the navy, common is what we called SOP: Standard Operating Procedure. *Common* is a trait shared by two or more individuals, a behavior that appears frequently, or a truth that is well known by a community.[1] We are groomed to be common by family, trained to toe the line in school, and cajoled to conform by peer groups and social media.

Let's face it, common is, well, the norm. It's perfectly acceptable to be common. But trust me on this: it is worth it to be uncommon. There is joy and freedom like you cannot imagine once you align your thoughts with your actions to live your unique and purpose-fueled life. To be uncommon, it is critical to rewire the fragmented and limited mindset you have been trained with. An uncommon mindset is integrated and exponential in capacity. Mastering innate physical, mental, emotional, intuitional, and spiritual intelligences, or what I call the *five mountains,* is the key to unlock this mindset. I've spent over three decades mastering my five mountains, allowing me to break free from the prison of a common, predictable life. Freedom isn't free and it takes work, but it is seriously worth it. I wrote this book to teach you how to master your five mountains so you can live the Uncommon Life too.

I know we are not all born equal in the sense that we're not all gifted with genius IQs like Marilyn vos Savant[2] or with the ability to compose music like Hans Zimmer. Few of us can draw like David Hockney, cook like Gordon Ramsay, or run like Lamont Jacobs.[3] Some of us know the square root of 324 off the top of our heads, but most of us have forgotten the basic multiplication tables by adulthood, as we're busy launching careers, paying bills, or raising kids. I admit to possessing none of the above abilities, in case you're wondering. But I have learned that though everyone can't be a prodigy, everybody does have vast, untapped potential. That potential lies within the mind, yet it remains dormant until one learns to break free. Break free from what? From the conditioning that is designed to keep you limited and dependent. Society's mental training system is customized to keep you trapped in common-land so it can feed off your money, time, and energy.

My mental training began with competitive swimming, which gave me a glimpse of my mind's power. Competitive sports enabled me to redirect my energy away from the partying during college and taught me how to control my breathing and to visualize success. These rudimentary skills played a crucial role in preparing me for the navy's Basic Underwater Demolition/SEAL (BUD/S) training that came a few years later. I'm grateful for the physical aptitude I was born with to be an athlete. That's because as I mastered my physical mountain, a glaring spotlight was pointed at the other mountains that needed tending—my mental, emotional, intuitional, and spiritual intelligences. Turning my attention to training these is what led to the breakthrough.

I found mental toughness through sports and endless hours in the wilds of upstate New York. There was no task I would not tackle, no workout or sucky thing I would not do. But though I was the quintessential badass on the outside, there was a persistent feeling of emptiness, of not being enough on the inside. I'm not so sure I would've recognized that void were it not for my physical and mental strength casting a light on a glaring emotional imbalance. The hollowness I felt left me searching constantly for direction, for purpose, and for true love. The hole in me felt like the size of the Grand Canyon. I fit the picture of perfection on the outside. On the inside, an aching panic was clinging to me like the faint scent of chlorine after training at Lineberry Pool at Colgate University.

I was only subtly aware of this existential struggle and couldn't grab onto it to study it closely. My family was averse to therapy in general and from my perspective lacked emotional awareness, let alone control. Emotional nuance was alien to my conditioned mind. So, I just ignored it, until I couldn't any longer.

So yes, I was a common kid who grew into a common man. I followed the rules impressed on me by my family, my schooling, and society. I was afraid to be different, to speak my truth and risk being cast out. I didn't know how to develop my inner strength beyond the basics of mental and physical toughness, so I accepted that living with chronic dissatisfaction was normal. Shame, negativity, jealousy, and self-questioning drove my behavior. I was convinced that true happiness was a fantasy or possessed by others somehow superior to me. I'd taken on the role of the overachiever yet was unraveling on the inside. My spirit was in a real slump.

Then, when I started my first career in Manhattan in 1985, I found meditation. After many hours training with this new tool, I received a life-changing sign from my intuition. No, it wasn't a double rainbow after a tough day or an apparition of my great-grandfather telling me I was special. It was an actual sign in a window—and it was pointing me toward an Uncommon Life, which was out there waiting. I just had to commit to the challenge.

And I did.

I will tell the rest of that story later.

Being uncommon means moving closer to the best version of yourself every day. It means living with focus, confidence, and humility. Being uncommon means learning how to communicate honestly and effectively. At this juncture in my personal journey, it means reaching more people than I did the day before. I'm a living embodiment of self-mastery and purpose, and nothing brings me joy like watching more and more people discover their paths to mastery and purpose. But I've read my book reviews, and I know I'm not everyone's cup of matcha. For every seven or eight that say, *"Mark's great!"* and that my programs have been life-changing, someone comments that I'm virtuous to the point of boring or that I can't relate to "real people" because my life is charmed. One reviewer actually said: *"This guy thinks he invented the wheel."*

I've learned to learn from the critics. No matter how hard I strive, I know there is no perfect. There are always going to be folks who neither appreciate nor grasp my philosophy. Some think that I'm just another one of those Navy SEAL authors shouting: "Toughen up, you loser!" (Nothing could be further from the truth.) Others will label me a dreamer for having the audacity to want to impact one hundred million people in the next twenty-five years (I state this on my personal website markdivine.com). And others might think

I'm a narcissist and living a fantasy. *Maybe I am . . . but* I can assure you that regardless of what anyone thinks of me, the value of becoming uncommon is well worth the effort. So why not go for it?

Accolades and awards are great but short-lived. To cultivate growth, we need to get real with ourselves and, sometimes, that means "reading the reviews." That's my first tip. Listening to my critics with an open heart has helped me to understand what's working and see where I can improve.

Here's the second tip: Don't take yourself too seriously. I'm going to teach you how to discern between constructive criticism and cruelty. This will help you develop emotional resiliency and hone your intuition while maintaining your sense of humor. It'll keep you going when the going gets tough.

Here's the third and final tip to get us rolling: There's always going to be someone on the sidelines telling you not to try something or that you're doing it wrong or that you'll never succeed. The wet blankets don't vanish into thin air once you achieve a goal, fall in love, make lots of money, or give it all away. Just know that the critics are those unwilling to do the hard work themselves. We must learn when to bend our ears and when to turn our backs . . . or risk losing focus.

I'm still a work in progress, just as you are. When I fall hard, I bleed the same. I just get up quicker, learn what went wrong, and carry on with a smile. And no, I don't think I invented the wheel (though, that would've been a nifty feat). But I've jumped through a lot of hoops and had thousands of special operators and other professionals to test my theories out on. I have failed and learned so many times so that you don't have to. I've trained my ass off in all five mountains, have followed the advice of world leaders, mentors, peers, coaches, therapists, and even my trainees. Bottom line, I've spent my life in pursuit of breaking free from common-land. This book is my attempt to reach 100 percent of the people willing to invest time and energy to become the best version of themselves possible in their lifetime. Yes, that's a lot of people and a lofty goal. Some might call it an impossible goal. *But you know what we're going to call it. . . .*

I want you to start thinking about your Uncommon Goals.

Inertia, from the Latin *iners,* meaning *lazy,* is the name for the tendency of an object in motion to remain in motion, or an object at rest to remain at rest, unless acted upon by a force. As we know, this is Newton's First Law of Motion and a quality that all objects made of measurable matter possess.[4]

Including humans.

Psychologists have a name for it. They call it *human iner- tia.*[5] Once we've established a life trajectory, we continue that path until acted on by a greater force.[6] We do this because it is comfortable, which is also mistaken for safe. And we do this despite the faint ache in our hearts and the nagging feeling in our guts that something is missing. We get comfortable, we get lazy, we listen to the voice in our head, ignore the yearn- ings of our heart, and stay the course.

Did you know it takes over 5,000 horsepower to move the average mainline locomotive from a stationary position, but it only takes around 30 horsepower to keep it going on a straight track at 130 miles per hour? This is the power of inertia.

The hardest part of any new self-development program is getting started. The second hardest part is getting comfortable with the discomfort of change. The third essential part is to keep going once you start. The shortest course in mental toughness is to not quit once you start something. You have started and are on your way. Now let's get comfortable being uncomfortable, and don't quit! This self-actualized Navy SEAL with decades of training under his belt (but no prodigious musical or mathematical talent whatsoever) will provide the blueprint to be uncommon and motivate you when you need it. You will beat the inertia of your common existence and change your life trajectory by following my training advice. That I can guarantee.

Welcome to your Uncommon Life.

Let's do this . . .

Easy day!

THE UNCOMMON CONTRACT

Are you ready for this? Ready to tap your *maximum potential, performance, and purpose,* to live free from fear and regret? Are you ready to take responsibility each day to evolve into the very best version of yourself? Are you ready to be:

- Healthier?
- More fit?
- More balanced?

- More focused?
- More clear-minded?
- More centered?
- More content?
- More peaceful?
- More truthful?
- More honorable?
- More connected?
- More whole?

The quality of your life is not about the size of your bank account, the length of your résumé, or the power you wield over others. It is a measure of your wholeness as a human and how you show up in service to others. It is expressed through the strength and balance of your physical, mental, emotional, intuitional, and spiritual domains.

Ask yourself if you are really ready now to commit to this work. It would be a fail to get temporarily inspired and then go back to being common. So, decide now that being common is a thing of the past.

You are going to have to trust me, this knowledge, and this path, at first. As your training takes root, you will prove it to yourself. If you do the work with a serious but light-hearted attitude, it will pay real dividends quickly. But mastery will take a lifetime.

You have one life to live, so why not be uncommon?

You deserve it.

I would like you to sign a binding contract for this work with your highest and best self.

I know what you're thinking: *You really want me to sign a contract to commit to this training?*

Yes, I do. If you aren't going to sign it physically, then do it mentally.

The SEALs made me sign a contract. And that contract became my "all in, all the time" commitment. That contract supercharged my motivation and growth. It requires a burn-your-boats level of commitment to get uncommon results.

Having that level of commitment toward your growth will cause you to up your game too. You will hold yourself to the highest standard, even and especially when the going gets tough.

> I, _____,
> commit to becoming uncommon. I will work the practices and exercises offered in this book until I have them mastered. If I waver, I will get back on track. If I take a break, I will recommit. I will not quit. This is worth it. Period.
>
> Signature: _____
> Date: _____

★ ★ ★

You must get comfortable with being uncomfortable to be uncommon. And when you do, you'll yearn and strive to stay in that zone.

Think about that.

This book is about climbing the five mountains of consciousness to self-mastery in service to others. There is no fluff in these pages, so proceed with an open heart, cautious optimism, and a mindset that's ready to do the work.

In Part I: Mastering Your Physical Mountain, we begin the journey by preparing our bodies to be as physically fit and healthy as possible for the climb.

Part I

MASTERING YOUR PHYSICAL MOUNTAIN

- We'll learn just how vital exercise is to maintain the health of both the body and brain.

- We'll learn that bad eating habits are more about mindset, less about willpower, and mostly about listening to our gut.

- We'll learn that human connection is as big an influence on quality of life and longevity as smoking and obesity are on decreasing lifespan.

- And I'll introduce you to journaling, breathwork, and visualization techniques to assist you in mastering your physical mountain.

1

THE POWER OF MOMENTUM

Considering modern man has been inhabiting the Earth for two hundred thousand years and civilization has been around for six thousand years (that we are aware of), we in the modern Western world haven't known about the benefits of exercise or nutrition for very long. It's been less than a century, to be exact, and the narrative about these important health drivers has been hijacked by commercial interests that don't profit from you gaining ultimate health freedom.

Women are even newer to the world of fitness and nutrition than men. It wasn't until 1984 that the Olympics held its first female marathon, where American underdog Joan Benoit Samuelson took the gold. Meanwhile, men had been playing professional sports for decades by that point.

Women, however, have a leg up on healthy living compared to men. Though the average lifespan of humans has been on a slow rise over the centuries, women have consistently out-aged men by an average of five years. According to Worlddata.com, women live seventy-four years on average to men's sixty-nine years. Scientists are just learning that having the same sex chromosomes (XX) in the DNA sequence creates an environment for optimal mitochondria functioning, giving the body the ability to produce more energy to create new cells and fight more aggressively against gene mutation, viruses, and disease. But also, behaviorally speaking, males tend to be less careful about their bodies, endure more physical stress than females, and avoid medical treatment. They also smoke more and consume more alcohol.[1] In the last few years, however, something's changed with both sexes: their average lifespans have dropped by two to five years.

This is sad but not surprising news.

While technology has done so much for science and medicine and to expand global interconnectedness, it has turned an active society idle. Our thumbs log more "steps" than our feet. Everything is automated and life has become too "done for you." The problem is that easy makes you weak. And being weak leads to unhealthy living, disease, and an early checkout.

A recent publication by the World Health Organization called physical inactivity a pandemic. It's now one of the leading causes of preventable death, up there with smoking and excessive alcohol use.[2] Obesity, the common denominator to almost all health-related diseases, is expected to hit 50 percent of the Western population by 2030. Due to this grave issue, WHO has created a document called the Global Plan of Action for Physical Activity 2018–2030, which outlines how to reverse the problem by the end of this decade in an effort to get life expectancy back on the rise.[3]

If you are shocked by these stats, you are not alone. Do you think we should be taking our health more seriously?

I do too.

Though the eighties were not all that long ago, Joan Benoit Samuelson said that as a teen she would avoid running on the road. She didn't like the looks she got, and she knew that her dream of becoming a marathon runner made her an outlier. She was going against the grain. Samuelson was uncommon.

Luckily, this is not the case anymore with exercise and athletics in most parts of the world. Male or female, young and old, working out is now more commonplace. And all the programs and details we could ever want on healthy living are just an app away.

There are simply no excuses to not move your body. It craves exercise and movement, so it's time to get moving if you are not already. Our lives literally depend on it.

I've put the five mountains in the order they are in for a reason. Physical activity and healthy living heal us from the inside out, strengthening the body and boosting mental health and emotional well-being. The aim is to make the body a fit vehicle for the mind to navigate the outer world effectively. The five mountains, when mastered, lead to a whole-mind, body-mind experience of expanded awareness. Move and improve the body, and the mind and heart will follow.

By "mastering your physical mountain," we're going to strengthen our bodies to be the foundation from which we propel up the five mountains of self-mastery.

Let's inoculate ourselves from the pandemic of poor health!

THE NEGATIVE SIDE OF POSITIVE ENERGY

We all know that we need to sleep seven to eight hours a night, eat right, and exercise regularly. We know lean protein and veggies are healthy and that hot fudge sundaes, greasy burgers, soda, and licorice ropes are poison. But we desire those things. And when we get stressed, bored, angry, frustrated, grief-stricken, lovesick, tired, lonely . . . we fall off the wagon and lose control of our minds. The idea is not to repress those emotions, desires, and fears—they're all a natural part of being human. The lack of mental toughness and emotional resiliency when those feelings come up is the real problem. And retraining your mind to think well is the cure.

In this third decade of the twenty-first century, our novel, everything-at-our-fingertips, fast-fueled, and tech-driven lifestyle has caused more of us to experience dis-ease and burnout than ever before. This common way of living is literally killing us. A large percentage of the population has become unhealthy slackers, though they are not likely to admit it. And despite innumerous breakthroughs in modern medicine, exercise, and nutritional sciences, overall health and global life expectancy is moving in the wrong direction!

Remember when you had to actually walk all the way across the room to get to the TV to change the TV channel? I bet most of you don't. (I guess I'm dating myself!) How odd that idea seems now . . . even just using a remote control seems like a chore. You misplace it and have to search high and low, cutting into downtime. Thank goodness we can now download a remote-control app on our phone.

Having the technological equivalent of a supercomputer in our hands 24-7 extends our mind's reach, but at the cost of laziness, poor attention control, and a negative impact on positive mindset. Also consider the effects of dopamine-triggering social media and doomscrolling network news. These are extremely negative and energy draining, but train people to stay dependent upon virtual connection and hyper-stimulation to feel a sense of aliveness. At one time, we connected to our vitality naturally by being outdoors, connecting with others, moving our bodies, and eating healthy food. As humans, we are meant to experience ample exercise, sunshine, play, and real food from the Earth—and we've been cut off from these essential elements of our own humanity.

One of my aims is to get people back to the way they should be living—back to doing real exercise, eating real food, and consuming real knowledge to shape their minds (as opposed to fear, disinformation, and control propaganda). If you are suffering from some of these challenges, whether as a result of the COVID-19 pandemic or simply due to the relentless societal drive toward ease and hyper-virtualization, then there is no time to waste in taking back your power right now. You will experience an immediate boost in positive energy, creative thinking, and overall health.

Since you're inspired to read this, you likely sense that

you're not living your best life in some way. So, there's no time like the present to do something about it. It's important to start your journey by nipping all the BS excuses in the bud. Below are a few of the biggest excuses I hear that hold people back from total physical and mental health, and subsequently, optimal performance:

1. I don't have the time or knowledge.
2. I don't have the money.
3. My kids consume my life.
4. I'm not able to stick to diets or train consistently.
5. I'm too burned out from my job to focus on bettering myself.
6. I always get injured, or I get bored when things get repetitive.

I can debunk each of these excuses one by one and show you how to overcome each one so you can start living up to your highest level of human potential.

1. I don't have the time or knowledge.

This one is simple: you don't need more time. If you can't fit thirty to forty-five minutes of physical activity into your schedule three to five times per week, then you've got serious time management problems. I have a cure for that too . . . as you'll see, time management problems are really commitment problems. And a lack of commitment comes from not being clear on your "why," which is a mental training problem. Fix the why, train the mind, and all else falls into place.

2. I don't have the money.

You also don't need money to get in shape. In 2018, I did 130,000 burpees and got in crazy shape. It didn't cost me a dime, just some mental focus. To train like that, you simply need more discipline, which is backed by that "why." Don't worry about the externalities, like looking as good as Arnold or being able to compete in the CrossFit Games. Those are weak, comparison-based motivators that won't serve your mind over the long term. Also, you don't need to turn your garage into a pricey Gold's Gym or aerial yoga studio. You don't even need to sacrifice a nice dinner out on the weekends to afford a gym membership, because you don't actually need one. Most of the best exercise and movement practices don't require expensive memberships or complicated equipment. My philosophy is that wherever you go, so goes your gym. Your best tools are your body and a floor, or better yet, the great outdoors. There are also thousands of programs and virtual coaches online if training in the cozy comfort of the indoors is your thing.

3. My kids consume my life.

I admit that being a parent can definitely suck a lot of your time and energy. I'm a parent, and I can tell you it is a lot more fun if you can run, do yoga, and play outdoors with your kids. I added my son to my workout routine and got pretty adept at doing push-ups with him on my back. He benefited immensely by observing me taking care of myself, as well as from my presence and playfulness. This is a huge win in the parenting department that will pay big dividends in later years. If you absolutely have no way of separating yourself from your kids (or from someone else in your care), then include them on the journey. You can also have your loved one help hold you accountable to your workouts.

4. I'm not able to stick to diets or train consistently.

Just because you've tried twelve diet plans in the last five years, it doesn't mean the next program you try will fail. The problem might be that you're expecting change to come from something outside yourself. Again, what is your "why"? Also, negative self-talk and negative body image will inhibit success every time. Self-inflicted mental and emotional abuse fosters inactivity, isolation, and depletes energy.

The research is clear that the physiological and mental benefits of exercise and healthy nutrition are a big factor in accelerating recovery from emotional and psychological imbalances. It is all upside—there are simply no adverse side effects to healthy living, no matter how off track you may be right now. The evil twin of negative self-talk is fear. Fear of failure and fear of discomfort are the main culprits in exercise program adherence. In an effort to appear perfect to others, we hold ourselves to impossible standards, and then quit when we realize we've set the bar too high. The problem is that we care too much about how others perceive us, thus we target the unobtainable to try to impress them. To succeed at attaining optimal health and performance, you must stop worrying about others. Start by focusing on developing your "why" and setting realistic goals. Perfectionism is a serious problem that I, too, suffered as a young adult. I had to learn to stop living in fantasyland and living for others. My "why" became to master myself to embody the traits of a Navy SEAL, and with that "North Star," I established appropriate goals to move toward it. I was challenged and motivated because it was a worthy goal. Day by day, in every way, stronger and better, hooyah-he!

5. I'm too burned out from my job to focus on bettering myself.

Task saturation is another big challenge. Our culture has trained us that it's good to overcommit. Just look at your own life for validation. It pains me to see overcommitted students or parents torturing their kids to build (or buy!) the perfect résumé for college applications. Perfectionism and keeping up with expectations of others can only lead to anxiety and disappointment. *Hyper-arousal* is the fancy name for burnout, and most of America is hyper-aroused. This is a fast track to failure, and I recommend you make a brutally honest assessment of your commitments (and stress level). Then begin to declutter your life and start to de-stress with a practice like box breathing. Take a hard look at where you've overcommitted. Learn to simplify your life to only take on what's *really* important and urgent. You'll find that much of what you've committed to is to impress someone else, or to fulfill an expected cultural role (such as being on the dreaded HOA board). But those are stories that aren't helping you to be uncommon, so you can deconstruct them. Overcommitting is almost always done because you haven't learned to say "no." This inability to say "no" stems from a fear of letting someone down, or not living up to a flawed image of what you are supposed to look like to others. Trust me, those "others" don't really care what you're doing—and if they do, then they need therapy.

6. I always get injured, or I get bored when things get repetitive.

Starting a new fitness regimen at a sprint is another sure way to fail. "Crawl, walk, and then run" is the training mantra in the SEAL teams. Overtraining and racing toward an imagined future are recipes for disaster. If you haven't worked out in three years, and suddenly you are cranking out SEALFIT workouts five days a week, then stand by for injuries or burnout. It sounds obvious, but I see this mistake all the time because folks want to see results fast. Be patient and learn to crawl before you run! Another problem I see is that one must "get in better shape" in order to start a serious functional fitness program, such as CrossFit or SEALFIT. The fastest path to success is to just start training (ideally with a coach), and then don't quit.

Once the newness wears off, exercise is mind-numbingly boring . . . right? Well, no, it doesn't have to be. I rarely do the same workout more than once. Constant variety and playfulness are the keys. But if your interest is an endurance sport like swimming or cross-country, then it can be boring until you develop the mental fortitude to quickly get into a flow state. Then you start to really enjoy the time spent in those formerly mind-numbing workouts. I was a competitive swimmer and can tell you that staring at the bottom of a pool for hours was a bit dull, but the mental strength I gained proved to be invaluable. My view now is that mono-structural exercise regimens, such as running or biking, are best as companions to a good functional fitness regimen. But if you love to compete and have trained your mind to enjoy the type of slog required for triathlons and ultra-endurance races, then this doesn't apply.

Training oneself to enjoy hard physical work is a long-term outcome of becoming uncommon. I don't recommend starting with a fifty-mile race like my nephew Dylan, now a Navy SEAL, did. That would be skipping right to the "run" phase of crawl, walk, and run. If an exercise is boring, you can try *stacked training,* which is a fancy term that means to learn something while you exercise. Listen to the latest episode of *The Mark Divine Show* while you work out, or geek out on any of the other great podcasts or audiobooks available these days. Stacked training can lead to deeper learning and more enjoyable training time if done with mindfulness. Make sure you take time to recover both the body and the brain after these sessions. This is important for healing the body and integrating the information for deeper learning.

My main point of debunking these excuses is this: to achieve uncommon health and fitness, you simply need to get started, keep it simple, and stick with it. All excuses stem from an untrained mind. The results will come with adherence to a plan and a lot of patience. Getting the body and brain fit is the foundation for all further growth. This baseline of optimal health should be nonnegotiable . . . no excuses.

If you are battling an illness or enduring a challenging

life situation where survival is the only goal, exercise may take a back seat. You need to do what you must to get out of the structural and environmental conditions blocking your path. Flee your war-torn country. Leave your abusive and dysfunctional relationship as a battered spouse. My words earlier are aimed at those who have the fortunate conditions to have freedom of time, movement, and opportunity. If that's you, then you're in the driver's seat. However, unless you are in that war zone, consider that you have created the stressful life circumstances by not maintaining a healthy lifestyle to begin with, by overcommitting, or by being generally unmotivated and disorganized. Beginning a disciplined exercise program is the most positive thing you can do for yourself to bring balance and structure into your life and to get your body-brain ready for deeper training.

We are masters of rationalization. We are born with this ability as sure as we are born with a nose on our face. Using one of these excuses over and over creates a mindset for failure.

Don't let your untrained mind sabotage your success by rationalizing or waiting for the perfect circumstances. That will keep you at average when you want to be on the road to self-mastery.

You know all this. But now you need an unbeatable strategy to blow past that voice in your head, the clever one with all the excuses and perfectly reasonable roadblocks. The ultimate secret weapon is effective mind training through my meditation techniques, which I will get to in the Mental Mountain section. But before that, let's dig deeper into why the physical mountain development is a prerequisite to all the others.

DEVELOP YOUR MOMENTUM SUPERPOWER

Tailoring your lifestyle to support your most important "why" goals is vital. Our environment is the people we surround ourselves with and the context we create for success (or not). This plays a significant role in whether we gain momentum toward our goals. And I cannot emphasize this enough: the best way to stay on target with any goal is to craft it carefully, write it down, and revisit it often. You don't need to draft a play-by-play of your day at the risk of creating so much structure that you cut off creativity and spontaneity. It is enough to take a few minutes in your morning ritual to log your most important personal training and professional targets, your fueling plan, and any emotionally challenging obstacles that may arise along the journey. The Unbeatable Planning Journal can help you stay on track with your daily ritual and goal planning. This level of daily "thinking about your thinking" will help you develop serious momentum power on the way to your new Uncommon Life.

SpaceX rockets require gargantuan effort and massive amounts of energy to launch—37 million horsepower to be precise. But once that rocket is in flight, it requires a fraction of that energy to keep moving. Recall that the average locomotive takes 5,000 horsepower to start from a dead stop to overcome the inertia that is the *starting resistance*. That's because what is called the *rolling resistance* is tiny compared to the starting resistance. They are pretty darn hard to slow down, too, once cruising along on autopilot. A panic stop for one of GE's 200-plus-ton locomotives is a half mile because, as you know, objects resist change to their state of motion.

This power of momentum can be put to beneficial use by you, too, when you adopt and sharpen new habits and patterns. The changes required to develop momentum toward your new goals require an outsized effort in the beginning . . . especially if you are starting from a dead stop. Yanking on your workout clothes three to five days a week, committing to journaling nightly—these things require you to overcome that gargantuan "starting resistance." But, once you've habituated the changes in routine and made them an indispensable part of your everyday rituals, you'll be cruising along with little effort. You'll feel the momentum and appreciate the progress as you become stronger and more energized. And you'll be able to look back, thanks to your journaling practice, to see the progress and adjust course when necessary. At this point, you'll have developed what I call momentum superpower. That comes when all the hard work and effort of starting and sticking to the early stages of the work is behind you. At that point you will find it untenable, almost impossible, to stop. This momentum will carry you effortlessly and relentlessly from that first worthy target to even loftier goals that become accessible to you because of your progress and new skills.

Now, before we move on to the first exercise, it is time to claim your secret weapon (if you are not doing it already) of box breathing. This is a technique I used to train SEAL candidates to allow them to remain calm and focused in times of stress. I recommend that this be practiced daily as part of your morning and evening rituals. We will also be starting every exercise introduced in this book with box breathing.

Box breathing is a controlled breathing practice that has profound benefits for health, arousal control, and mental regulation (i.e., the ability to focus and make good decisions while under pressure). The practice is done through the nostrils bringing in as much air as possible without causing stress. Simply inhale, hold the breath, exhale, and then hold it again. Do each breath and each hold to a three-, four-, or five-second count (whichever is most comfortable to you, it is not a competition). The ideal prescription is to box breathe for twenty minutes in the morning and again in the evening. It can also be done as a spot drill a couple of times during the day for shorter durations. My team and I do it before every meeting. You can start at a crawl with five minutes and work your way up. If you'd like a guided video, here's a link to one for your convenience: https://unbeatablemind.com/boxbreathing. We also have a box breathing app you can find at https://boxbreathing.org.

Congrats! The power of momentum has gotten you through the first chapter, and you're ready to do the work!

EXERCISE 1
Start Your Journal and Your Journey

Joan Benoit Samuelson says you should think about your running in minutes, not distance. She believes in balance. *"Sports cannot be all-consuming. You have to balance the mind, body, and spirit."* After more than five decades in athletics, she still has a passion for it, thanks to living by this philosophy.[4] It's important that you feel this way, too, about your new Uncommon Life. So, whatever your choice of exercise, if this kind of discipline is new to you, I'd like you to commit to micro goals and not try to run fifty miles in your first session. Just twenty minutes per day, three times per week, will put you on the path to greatness. Determination and discipline will win over skill and natural talent over the long run. No excuses, just do it.

With the *Unbeatable Journal* (available only at Amazon) you will be able to up your game like Joan by journaling what I call the "Six Pillars of Optimal Performance." These are six critical areas you need to dial in new habits to put you, and keep you, on target and motivated for optimal health, fitness, and performance. You can start now to assess yourself in each of the six areas, then pick one new habit a month to implement from each pillar to build serious momentum superpower. The Six Pillars of Optimal Performance recommendations include, but are not limited to:

Physical Movement and Exercise

- Perform a minimum of twenty minutes of functional movement or cardiovascular exercise three to five days a week.
- Do somatic movement (yoga, chi gong, range of motion, etc.) for a minimum of five minutes every morning.
- Do short spot drills of fifty squats, burpees, or pushups during the day.

Fueling and Nutrition

- Carry fresh water with you and drink half your body weight in ounces every day.
- Eat natural, high-quality foods 80 percent of the time.
- Eat 30 percent less than what you have been trained to eat.
- Intermittent fast (the easiest way to eat less!).
- Cut out the sugary and high carb snacks.

Sleep and Recovery

- Do yoga or stretching movements every morning and after every workout.
- Schedule active recovery and days of rest in your training plan.
- Plan for between seven and eight hours of sleep. Track it with an Oura Ring or your watch.
- End eating, drinking any alcohol, and any electronic stimulation two hours before bedtime.
- Black out your room and consider using a cooling device such as Eight Sleep.

Stress and Mental Management

- Practice five or more minutes of box breathing daily (building up to twenty minutes).
- Read something inspiring as part of your morning or evening ritual, or a spot drill.
- Say no to new commitments and say yes to downtime for learning or helping someone out.

Time in Nature

- Get outside every day to walk, breathe, get some direct sunlight, and clear your head.

- Spend longer times in nature camping, hiking, or traveling.
- Get direct sunlight as soon as you wake up. Your circadian rhythm is set by this, with sleep occurring roughly sixteen hours later.

Communities of Practice and Learning

- Don't be a lone ranger in your learning and growth.
- Build or join one or more communities of practice. Examples include groups of peers committed to growth such as a martial art, yoga, art, chess or book club, any outdoor activity, improv or acting class, or learning anything new that inspires you.

I like to journal progress on these in the evening. Begin by answering the following questions:

- What went well today?
- What did not go well?
- What can I learn about what went well, and what can I change about what did not?
- What negative habit is holding me back?
- What new habit will I commit to, and how/when?

You only need a few minutes a day for a journaling practice, and it is essential for growing your self-awareness. It was Socrates who said that an unexamined life is not worth living. That sounds harsh, but if you consider that without deeply examining your mental training and reconstructing new, uncommon stories to guide your behavior and goals, then you are blissfully (or painfully) ignorant that you are dancing to someone else's tune. If you're not in love with the idea of daily introspection with morning and evening rituals, then I urge you to give yourself thirty days to prove that it is as invaluable as I claim.

In the next chapter, we'll look at the benefits of exercise that are not as obvious as sporting a new six-pack but are key to improving brain function, living free from pain and injury, and increasing longevity.

2

MOVE THE BODY, GROW THE MIND

Extraordinary French pianist Colette Maze began recording for the first time in her nineties. In the fall of 2021, she released her sixth album. At the age of one hundred and seven, Maze says that "tickling the ivories every day" is what keeps her young. And she adds that practicing the piano at her age is "no more complicated than eating a salad."

World-renowned artist and dancer Eileen Kramer, at one hundred and six, was still working as a choreographer in Sydney, Australia, until the pandemic forced her indoors. This is when she discovered her inner writer, publishing *Elephants and Other Stories* in June of 2021, a quirky and wise collection from her observations on life.

Known as the Father of Fitness, the late Jack LaLanne pulled himself out of an adolescence riddled with sugar, stomach issues, headaches, and mood swings. A lecture on nutrition that his mother dragged him to changed his life.

He went on to fuel his body with whole foods after that and made exercise a way of life. His dis-eases disappeared, including his need for glasses. Well into his eighties, LaLanne devoted two hours daily to exercise. He lifted weights for an hour and spent another hour swimming. If you're not familiar with this icon, you should look up some of his athletic feats, which have been referred to as nothing short of magical in the days when extreme sports were unknown . . . such as towing seventy rowboats with seventy people on board attached to a rope held in his mouth while swimming in San Francisco Bay on his seventieth birthday!

These legends help make the case that physical and cognitive declines, including memory loss, are not an inevitable outcome of aging. In my research, I have come across many accounts of yogis and martial arts masters living so long that their age was forgotten even to themselves. Even today, many masters have the physical body of a fifty-year-old well into their hundreds. These individuals are unknown to the Western world for two reasons: First, they avoid contact with modern culture to prevent the negative energy drain, and second, Western academics and scientists simply refuse to believe in this possibility. I, however, am greatly inspired by the practices of optimal living leading to an uncommonly long and healthy life. The postmodern model of the aged individual deteriorating away in a nursing home, eating applesauce and watching the boob tube, is a sad and unnecessary path. The "normal aging" process, when optimized around the six pillars, and combined with skillful mental training, is a pleasant and empowering experience. With these tools and some discipline, mental and physical attributes will improve as you age, albeit with different skills in your older days than your younger years.

If you're an athlete, martial artist, painter, chess aficionado, pianist, gardener, crossword puzzle fiend, etc., aging doesn't affect your ability to do the things you've always done . . . if you keep working on improving them. For those of you who are master debaters, your ability to argue and reason doesn't vanish when you hit seventy, eighty, ninety, or beyond. Uncommon sense does not diminish with age, nor does your physical health have to. If you were absent the day God handed IQ out, aging won't make it magically appear, but mental training can. Life experiences combined with your mental training will allow for a rich inner world to open and come more alive than your everyday experiences. More insight, wisdom, and mental power accrue through the years as you live an examined life.

All things being healthy, the brain is equipped for longevity if the body and mind are kept strong. It is part of the negative social training system that says that as people hit fifty or sixty they will start slowing down and the decline picks up steam from there. And when mental decline occurs with no diagnosis of a brain degenerative disorder, it's chalked up to "the normal aging process"—which I believe is not normal at all.

In this next section, I will investigate how adhering to an integrated training plan literally makes the brain a younger, bigger, faster, stronger, calmer taskmaster as you age biologically. The older your body becomes, the younger your mind can become. And the earlier you start, the better the long-term results.

YOUR BRAIN ON EXERCISE

Weight loss, better quality sleep, enhanced mood, increase in muscle mass, increase in joint strength and flexibility, reduction in body fat: we know that effective fueling and exercise achieves these things. But regular cardiovascular activity and strength training can affect other physiological conditions that you may have never considered:

- Exercising is one of the most effective ways to improve concentration, memory, and mood. But did you know it can also reduce the symptoms of attention-deficit/hyperactivity disorder (ADHD)? Drugs such as Ritalin boost the brain's dopamine, norepinephrine, and serotonin levels to create focus. Prolonged physical exertion sends a message to the brain to release those exact same hormones but without the negative side effects of the pharmacological interventions.
- The University of Georgia did a study published in *Psychotherapy and Psychosomatics* that proved as little as twenty minutes of cardiovascular activity three days a week for six weeks combats fatigue, because increasing your heart rate increases blood flow, which carries more oxygen and nutrients to your muscles. The oxidative stress that occurs in muscle cells from exercise can trigger mitochondrial biogenesis,[1] producing more adenosine triphosphate (ATP). Tada! More energy.[2]

- Regular exercise promotes structure and organization in your life. A regular workout routine keeps you grounded in times of stress and even turmoil. It's the one healthy thing you can *always* do for you.

- Getting ready for a workout—putting on comfortable, breathable, colorful attire—can boost your confidence. Similar to my teammate Admiral McRaven's admonishment to "make your bed" every day, doing a positive act toward your optimization first thing every day builds serious momentum power. Donning your "athleisure attire" first thing signifies "I am fit, training is what I do!"[3] Don't underestimate the power of the outfit to help stay "in fit."

- Exercise can reduce the symptoms and duration of being stuck in a state of fear and panic due to post-traumatic stress and other trauma. PTS toggles our nervous system into hyper-arousal, which is immobilizing. Exercise, especially involving bi-lateral movements that engage both arms and legs, can turn that switch off and get the central nervous system functioning normally again. Walking (especially in sand or snow) is an effective crossbody exercise. So are running, swimming, weight training with free weights, martial arts, dancing, hiking, rock climbing, biking, and skiing.[4] Combine exercise with mental training, proper fueling, sleep, recovery, nature time, and learning new things and you have a recipe for excellence.

- As mentioned, the research is now clear that routine exercise combats memory loss and age-related decline.

The same endorphins that make you feel better and increase focus (serotonin, dopamine, and norepinephrine) also stimulate the neuroplastic growth of new brain cells.

- Strength training can help improve something called *cognitive flexibility,* which is your ability to switch between tasks as well as recover resiliently when confronted with a challenge.[5]

The most important fact is this: it is a myth that cognitive decline and physical weakness comes with aging. How you develop lifestyle habits now will have an enormous impact on how the body-brain ages. We can produce new brain cells and improve our mind's clarity and focus until we die. One way to do this is to take on daily meditation, along with new learning challenges, be it chess, the ukulele, a foreign language, knitting, or by becoming a writer at the age of one hundred and six. New skills, practiced repeatedly, stimulate brain growth. But your brain also depends on cardiovascular activity to stay mentally acute and even grow.[6] The "move it or lose it" idiom doesn't just apply to maintaining that fit and ferocious figure. The Uncommon six pillar habits introduced earlier will preserve your physical and cognitive skills, protect your gray matter, and produce more brain cells. Honing the six pillars also strengthens your immune system, making you more resistant to pathogens and debilitating injuries.

Doctors, scientists, and the media go on and on nowadays about the benefits of exercising to keep your body and heart healthy, and they're right. But let's continue to examine the positive effects that exercise has for the brain.

- For those of you who wake up groggy, exercise can literally clear your head by strengthening neural receptors.
- Activities that require extra coordination and focus, such as learning the salsa, rock climbing, or trail running all stimulate the production of genes that belong to a class of growth factors called *brain-derived neurotrophic factor* (BDNF) proteins, which stimulate new neuronal connections and neurogenesis.[7]
- If you're older and you're feeling forgetful, regular cardiovascular activity will increase the size of your hippocampus, upping your flexible cognition, navigating skills, and your ability to form and retrieve memories.
- Stress releases cortisol, which hinders neurogenesis. Exercise reverses that process.

Consistency in your daily physical training is key to maintaining and sharpening your mind. It's clear how the brain responds to physical fitness activity. Now let's look in detail at how it reacts to fueling with different foods.

YOUR BRAIN ON FOOD

The human brain is roughly 2 percent of total body mass but uses 20 percent of the body's available energy to operate.

Think about that. Twenty percent of your nutritional intake is used to fuel 2 percent of your body! And the quality of that nutrition has a huge impact on the functioning of the brain. This should be motivation enough to think carefully about what fuel to put into the body's fuel tank. The body and brain operate at their peak when fueled with foods high in lean protein, vitamins, antioxidants, and monounsaturated fats. On the other hand, fueling with typical fast food and packaged food options filled with refined sugar and processed carbohydrates is a recipe for ill health, poor performance, and degenerative "age-related" diseases.

With all the evidence so clearly presented, you can no longer ignore the role that food plays in your ability to think, reason, focus, and maintain a state of mental well-being.

Though the brain is a real energy hog, if you think about it, 98 percent of our total body mass is affected by the rest of the energy we consume.

We are all creatures of habit. We find comfort in routine and avoid discomfort like the plague. This is the power that human inertia has over us.

If you haven't developed a love for exercise and clean eating (yet) and your routine includes processed food and inactivity (because you are too stressed and fatigued to work out), then you are likely in that group of nearly 50 percent of people who have unhealthy weight. This positive energy balance (when energy intake is greater than energy expenditure) means it is normal to seek out those same comforts in food and idle distractions in times of stress—which is all the time because you are in a state of hyper-arousal. This is a

vicious negative cycle that is difficult to get out of and is killing you slowly. Your go-tos, however unhealthy, are soothing.
They are familiar. But they are just short-term fixes creating
a long-term deadly problem. A good example of a short-term
fix with long-term health effects is the late-night fridge binge.
You don't consider that you are hungry because you are out
of balance and awake due to elevated cortisol. You eat whatever looks good, then go to sleep disappointed in yourself,
ballooning from bloat and regret. Add momentum to the
negative cycle as you fast-forward to the next evening, and
there you are staring into the fridge like a deer in the head-
lights. Again. This goes on night after night, year after year.

Cognitive Behavioral Theory (CBT) states that recogniz-
ing and acknowledging the negative impact of our choices
and habits is the first step to changing them. We know that
it is important to eat healthy foods and in reasonable quanti-
ties. We also know that we should be exercising regularly and
sleeping seven to eight hours a night. We now understand the
effect not doing these things has on our brains. It's not good.
Convert this vicious cycle to a "virtuous" lifestyle cycle with
some simple shifts in your thinking about fueling. Food intake is the most crucial of the six pillars. "Garbage in, garbage
out" means junk food intake leads to no energy to put out.
Those poor food choices lead to no energy for exercise, which
leads to poor sleep and greater stress. The vicious cycle starts
with poor thinking, which leads to poor fueling choices, and
the downward cycle picks up steam from there. So, it is crucial
to understand *why* we desire certain foods at a subconscious
level. If 2 percent of our body is using 20 percent of our fuel

intake, it stands to reason the brain plays a very important role in what we eat, when we eat, and why we eat. So, when we want to "go on a diet" or switch out bad eating habits for healthy ones, we need to look at changing the way we think about food and the whole process of fueling our system.

HOW THE BRAIN FEELS ABOUT FOOD

The hypothalamus, the organ at the base of the brain, houses a center called the *appestat*. This center is believed to control appetite. It has an internal gauge that determines satiety, that feeling of being satisfied from eating. But the more we eat, the higher the setting goes, so more food is required to trigger that feeling of being satisfied. This gauge plays a much bigger role in weight issues than calories.

The need to eat starts with a stimulus (hunger pangs or a thought about food). This is followed by the brain immediately activating a sensation of desire for food, which is then gratified with consumption until the gauge in the appestat is back to neutral.

If this is a nonscheduled eating period, then afterward, the mind rationalizes and justifies why it ate. If it's planned, such as one of our three "square meals" a day, then it's a no-brainer and we let ourselves off the hook if we overdo it. But when we gorge on junk just because we feel that sensation to eat, we will beat ourselves up, sending more negative energy throughout our bodies. And the excuses pile up to get off the hook from feeling guilty, and the rationalization is that *I'll do better to-*

morrow. That statement generally ends the argument. Until tomorrow.

In his book, *Healing and Recovery,* psychiatrist, physician, researcher, and spiritual teacher Dr. David Hawkins[8] tells us: *"Our thoughts and beliefs about weight, activity, calories, and all the phenomena surrounding this have been affecting our weight. It is necessary to reverse the conventional, so-called 'common sense' of the left-brain logic that says it is the body that creates the mind. Instead, we have to look at the opposite, which is that what is held in mind manifests within the body."*[9]

Dr. Hawkins understood that there is a difference between the body needing fuel for survival and the brain telling the body to eat for myriad emotional reasons, including anxiety, cravings, and boredom. And once we distinguish between the genuine need for food and those other sensations, we can begin to control our eating habits through cognitive behavioral change in habits. The body will trick you until it is rebalanced. And the mind is trained to listen to the body. Start to pay attention to the conditioning and interrupt the patterns that lead to unhealthy choices. But who is paying attention to the brain that is out of control? The unconscious mind is conditioned from childhood to react to the body and other external stimulus. But your higher self, your all-knowing heart's wisdom center, or soul if you will, knows what's best. It is time to start listening to that.

We've all heard "you are what you eat," and this is true in the sense that your body will be shaped by what you eat. But I want you to start thinking that what you eat is a result of not just what you think, but how you think. The inability to control appetite is not just about having little willpower. This is why CBT alone falls short. We need to evaluate and adjust unhealthy eating habits at the source—long before the bingeing occurs. You will manage the desires, cravings, and emotional eating in the unconscious mind, which then shapes the conscious mind to make better cognitive (overt and conscious) choices, which in turn shapes your body for an Uncommon Life.

Practically speaking, there are numerous ways to begin the cognitive behavioral "conscious" level of retraining the brain from overeating:

- Slow down when you eat.
- Don't eat when you're distracted by the TV or anything else.[10]
- Manage stress using a tactic other than food, and practice that new habit till it's done unconsciously.
- Stop eating before bedtime and after. Ideally you will eat or drink nothing for two hours before sleepy time. If you eat, you will stimulate the release of the hormone cortisol, which will interrupt your sleep. Cortisol also stimulates fat and carbohydrate metabolism, making you hungry, oftentimes craving salt and sugar. Too much cortisol also offsets testosterone production. This can cause a decrease in muscle mass, which reduces the number of calories your body burns. This weight gain often happens in the belly region, increasing the risk for cardiovascular disease.[11]
- Regular exercise reduces overeating by creating a stronger mindset, one that leads to healthy food choices because the body is telling the brain that it feels better.

- Eating too much sugar confuses the brain, and it fires off false signals about hunger. Decreasing sweets, simple carbs like bread and cereal, and other foods with high-fructose corn syrup turns that signal down.

- The biome is a big contributor to unconscious fueling habits. Gut bacteria can affect how different foods are digested and produce chemicals that create the feeling of hunger or satiety. Fiber and plants (flavonoids) help manage weight due to the role of gut bacteria in the digestion process sending a message of satisfaction.[12] Sometimes, just being aware when you have an emotional craving versus being hungry will help you differentiate and stop a bad habit.

- The sedentary lifestyle of our modern-day lives, especially in urban populations, has put our body into a state of needing less food than we did even two decades back. But because our brain has not caught up with this fact, and we are peppered with subconscious programming from the big, packaged food industry, we generally overeat as a cultural habit. This even goes for the caloric intake of the pets that share our homes. They're eating the same amount as they've always been but exercising less too! Our pets have fallen victim to our laziness, reducing their lifespans. If your pet is a big motivator for you, then change the habits for both of you!

When I was in the SEALs, we did not pay attention to food choices like they do today. I was in the habit of jamming whatever I could get my hands around into my mouth after sixteen hours of training. We trained so hard and long that we would, and could, eat anything . . . pizza and beer being my favorite food group. We didn't know then about the importance of eating whole foods or about paleo and keto diets or about the benefits of intermittent fasting. We just ate because we needed the calories, but it took its toll eventually. I've since habituated myself to avoid most processed foods, especially anything with refined sugar, and white bread and pasta products. Also, I eat only two meals a day between 11:00 A.M. and 6:00 P.M. Intermittent fasting has been shown to enhance brain health and longevity.

Intermittent fasting is an eating pattern where you cycle between periods of eating and fasting. This style of fueling may compel the body to use fat stores in the liver, inducing the production of ketones. Studies have shown this metabolic switch also coincides with better brain function and offers protection from oxidative stress.[13] Longer fasts of twenty-four hours or so are also an excellent means to reduce caloric intake and cleanse the body-brain from a buildup of toxins. The longer fasts also have an emotional quality to them as they allow you to access emotions often numbed with food. Further, fasting spiritual vision quests have been employed by Native traditions for centuries to develop insight and induce spiritual states, which also equate to psycho-emotional development.

One final note about brain health. Most people are exposed to some form of brain trauma from accidents, sports, or occupations. Studies reveal that military service can expose one to blast trauma from blowing stuff up, micro-trauma from weapons firing, and the like. Football, rugby, boxing, martial arts, soccer, skateboarding, surfing, and any situation where your head gets conked repeatedly, or you experience a concussion is *no bueno* for the brain. The impacts bounce your brain around in your skull, creating bruising that limits blood flow. Many times you will not notice, such as with routine micro-traumas. But even if you knock yourself out and heal from short-term memory loss, the long-term effects can lead to dementia, anxiety, and other post-traumatic stress in later years. My work with veterans has really opened my eyes to the severity of this problem. I did a podcast with Dr. Daniel Amen, author of *Change Your Brain, Change Your Life*, who believes that these traumas can be healed with dietary changes, supplementation, exercise, and hyperbaric chamber treatments. This information is not "brain science," it simply reinforces the obvious fact that if you want to optimize the functioning of the body and brain, then you need to optimize the six pillars that keep them tuned up daily. I acquired a hyperbaric chamber in 2021 and use it regularly for recovery and to ensure that my brain is functioning well. You should be thinking about all this now . . . not just when it shows up as a problem in later years.

All choices, behaviors, and unconscious reactions originate as thoughts in our minds, impacted not just by our psychology but also our physiology. The connection between mind and body is impossible to deny. So, to optimize thinking and behavior, we work on both simultaneously. The physical mountain is the first to climb because it is foundational to the other four. Get the body and brain in order, and working on the mental, emotional, intuitional, and spiritual mountains is made possible. Now, we're going to do a simple visualization technique to train for your new fueling choices and workout habits to achieve the fit body and brain you deserve.

EXERCISE 2
Visualize Your Ideal Body

PART 1:

Start with five or more minutes of box breathing.

Now, we're going to familiarize ourselves with a very simple visualization exercise. We will do more sophisticated imagery exercises in the upcoming chapters, but this will be a nice start.

Project into the future three to five years, and imagine your body as extremely healthy and fit, radiating energy. It is looking good and feeling good. You are outside doing some exercise, play, or work and engaged with others with a high sense of self-esteem, love, and connection. You feel whole, grateful, and peaceful. This is your "ideal self," and visualizing it will create a mental representation that acts the same way as a memory of a past mental representation of yourself does. Over time, as you practice this new self-image in your mind, you will have more motivation and subconscious prompting to take action and make behavioral modifications that will ensure it comes true. Make sure it's realistic. For example: don't imagine yourself three inches taller.

1. Register the feelings that come up. You should feel more relaxed, motivated, and empowered. Allow the feelings of self-love or peace to be embodied and relax into this new version of yourself.
2. A few minutes of this is fine. When done, just let the imagery slip away and come back to the present. This is a good time to journal about your future self to reinforce the experience. You have to see something in your mind to believe it, and then make it happen.

This is your true future self.

Whenever you feel down or are questioning your physical body, pause, breathe deeply, and bring up that image and feel the positive emotions. This will energize you and remotivate you. With that image in your mind, there's also no space for negative self-talk. This exercise helps to eradicate poor body habits at the source—in your mind where they originate. When practiced consistently, the mind will automatically begin to move in that direction . . . and the body will follow.

PART 2:

Here's a list of simple six-pillar habits to keep your body and brain in the game. I've already picked one from each category for you back in Exercise 1 (those are crossed out for your convenience). Begin to add them to your training arsenal to build your momentum superpower.

- ~~If you're new to exercise, do twenty or more minutes of cardiovascular physical training three to five days a week (or forty minutes if you're already an established exerciser.)~~
- Do some spinal and somatic movement for five minutes every morning.
- Make time for spot drills of squats and push-ups a couple times a day.
- Get seven to eight hours of sleep a night.
- Carry fresh water with you and drink it throughout the day.
- Do an inventory of your food intake and begin to eliminate the sugar-laden crap.
- Box breathe every morning and before any stressful event.
- ~~Practice five or more minutes of box breathing daily (building up to twenty minutes).~~
- Read something inspiring for five to twenty minutes (or more) every day.

- Volunteer to do new things or try new things. Say "yes" to helping. It's as simple as that.
- Begin to learn the first most important skill you will need for your new mission.
- Get outside every day to walk, breathe, and clear your head.
- Join a community of like-minded people doing something healthy—such as ju-jitsu, yoga, mountain biking, or join a hiking group or a book club. We will discuss in the next chapter just how important it is to not go it alone.

In the third and final chapter of Mastering Your Physical Mountain, we're going to learn about the awesome power of connection. The work you've committed to by signing the Uncommon Contract tells me you're ready. You've created a strong sense of purpose, and the vision for where you want to go is becoming clearer. The commitment to getting there will give you tremendous motivation, and the power of connection will keep you on track!

3

TEAMWORK MAKES THE DREAM WORK

n the 1985 NFL draft, the San Francisco 49ers took a gamble on an unknown athlete from a small college in Mississippi. A year later, wide receiver Jerry Rice started making football history. By the time he retired, he'd broken more than a hundred records and played in eight conference championships and four Super Bowls, winning three.[1] Nicknamed The G.O.A.T. (Greatest Of All Time), Rice takes little credit for his success. Instead, it was the team of his father, a brickmason, who taught him the importance of hard work and humility, and his high school principal, who pushed him to try football after noticing his speed darting down the hall after getting caught skipping class. He's also grateful for teammate Tim Brown of the Raiders. Under new head coach Bill Callahan, they became the greatest receiving duo in team history. And Rice says his chiropractor's magic kept him aligned and unbroken over the course of his record-breaking twenty-season career.[2]

Stanford all-American, Major League Soccer player, and international superstar Bobby Warshaw wrote in a 2013 *PennLive Patriot News* article that his success on the soccer field is in large parts the result of playing for countless hours in the yard with his brothers, to his youth soccer coach for letting him compete with the older kids, to his guidance counselor for helping him balance school and sports, to his high school coach for teaching him to grow up, and to his parents . . . for a million other things. Warshaw says he has never done anything alone. *"My life is a crazy conspiracy of the world coming together. . . . I have not only my strength, but the strength of thousands of people who have shaped me."*[3]

In the 2022 Tokyo Olympics, tennis underdog Markéta Vondroušová, ranked forty-first in the world, beat number-one-ranked star Naomi Osaka in the third round of women's singles. The Czech Republic player found herself up against Belinda Bencic of Switzerland, ranked ninth, and wound up with the silver. No one predicted either athlete would be battling for the gold.[4] Both players' fathers introduced them to tennis as toddlers and cultivated their love of the game.

Jerry Rice, Bobby Warshaw, Markéta Vondroušová, and Belinda Bencic didn't find success on their own. They did it thanks to the love, sacrifice, and support of family and community. And from my world, they called us the "SEAL Teams" for a reason. We would have failed miserably had we been the "SEAL Individuals!" Teamwork really does make the dream work.

"There is no such thing as a self-made person. You will reach your goals only with the help of others," said George Shinn, former owner of the Charlotte, and New Orleans, Hornets. Shinn credits team sports for getting him through high school when he wasn't academically inclined and his widowed mom was struggling to make ends meet.[5]

Every true competitor, successful entrepreneur, artist, or even Navy SEAL has a list a mile long of people who helped make their unique goals a reality. We can't do life alone, not to the level of greatness and self-mastery that our true self knows is possible.

ALL IN, ALL THE TIME

Some might say I was born to be a SEAL. But I had to work hard to habituate the thoughts and actions that enabled me to thrive in the most intense and dangerous military training in the world. Sure, I went into the program in great shape (just like every other recruit). But I had to step up my game to levels beyond college athletics, and it was because of my small team (boat crew) of six, amongst the 184 other recruits, that I discovered extraordinary potential to become the Honor Man of Class 170. Then, once I entered the SEALs, I had to work even harder with the Alpha Platoon team to propel me as an elite Spec Ops leader. Yes, I worked my butt off in training. But I would not have succeeded without my teammates and mentors.

To get to, and operate at, peak performance, we need to

physically work with others to gain a mental and emotional edge. Those others will include parents, coaches, teammates, mentors, therapists, or a best friend who eggs you on to be better than you are allowing yourself to be. Oftentimes those on your team are not even aware of it, as when you are inspired by a great book and read it ten times, dog-earing and underlining the most inspiring parts.

But searching for and relying on a team does not come naturally, especially in a culture built on staunch individuality. And due to inertia, optimal performance is the harder path, so it takes constant and never-ending persistence and motivation. It takes time to build that motivation internally. Even the motivated few get sidetracked by the circumstances of life and, suddenly, eight hours of sleep, healthy eating, and exercise are the first to go from the daily routine.

Why is this the case? What is the missing link?

For those who aren't impressed by case studies on lab rats or spooked by the notion that three or four decades from now you might become forgetful and regret not having worked out daily, let's get you on course by using another, more powerful means of motivation. For everyone else, this will keep you on course and assist you in reaching, and exceeding, your uncommon goals.

EMBRACE THE SUCK TOGETHER

We all know how to take good care of ourselves by now: eat right, work out, get enough sleep. But let's talk about the role human connection plays in our well-being and ability to thrive.

In 2010, an influential meta-analysis of social isolation and its effect on mortality, using 148 separate case studies with three hundred participants over seven years, determined that a lack of social connection is a greater risk factor to health than smoking, obesity, and high blood pressure.[6] The study further revealed that strong social connections strengthen our immune system, help us recover from illnesses faster, lower anxiety and depression, increase self-esteem and empathy for others, create trust, cooperation, and generate an interpersonal feedback loop of "social, emotional, and physical well-being."[7] And strong social connections can lead to a 50 percent increased chance of longevity. The buddy system increases our lifespan! This study has been backed by numerous since, which have rendered the same results.

Even as little as three hundred years back, living to age thirty-five was considered the norm. Advancements in science and medicine have been credited with the drastic jump in lifespan in the twentieth century, but we are learning that human connection has played a major role too—especially now that we are seeing the effects of the reversal of this connection with what's been called the *isolation crisis*.

Social connectedness has been dropping since the early 2000s. In the eighties, the average adult claimed to have three close friends. Today, a large percentage of Americans say they have only one person to confide in, with 25 percent claiming to have no one.[8] It's safe to assume, if isolation is as detrimental to our health as smoking and physical inactivity, then it's one of the culprits responsible for our decrease in health and longevity. We simply must change this! And I'm not just talking to boomers, millennials, or Gen Zers. Our youth are more socially isolated than ever, and more sedentary. We all need to connect more, on behalf of our health and longevity as well as for future generations. We must lead by example, and the most effective way to do this, based on the stats, is through exercising together with a swim buddy (that's what we called our accountability partner in the SEALs), group, or team.

Finding a support system as you embark on your journey up the physical mountain is vital to your success because it means you've gone public with your goal. It's out there. No turning back now. Shit just got real.

You're not going to hit the snooze if your swim buddy is waiting for you at the gym. You don't want to be the person who no-shows or can't keep their word or becomes known as the flake. It's one thing to lie to yourself with all those left-brained rationalizations—it's another to lie to a coach or friend.

It's human nature to collaborate to survive and to thrive. For almost all human history, we've been hunter-gatherers, relying on community and sharing in basic, common goals. Banding together meant staying alive.[9] You had to pull your weight. People counted on you. It sometimes meant the difference between life and death.

In today's times, your workout partner isn't likely to die of malnutrition or a spear to the heart if you blow off your Monday morning trail run. But being a disappointment stings just enough that we try to avoid it. It triggers guilt and self-loathing and a string of negative self-talk. It breaks trust. And people lose faith in you.

For those reasons and more, having a person or team that relies on you creates responsibility and breeds trust. Account-ability becomes the razor-sharp knife that carves the grooves of a new routine into your lifestyle faster than even journal-ing can. Writing down your goals makes you accountable to "you." Involving others on this journey makes you account-able to your destiny. Having backup has played out time and again in my own life. I owe so much to so many.

But keep in mind, if you're part of a team, you adopt their ways, good and bad. That is what a cultural norm is.

If you get involved in small group training at your local gym and everyone gossips, it's more likely than not that you'll fol-low suit, even if you feel bad about it afterward. If you play in a men's rec hockey league and everyone goes out for beers and burgers after the matches, even those who don't love drinking will probably partake. A family is a team. Your coworkers are a team. There are all kinds of teams in your life. Are they benefit-ting you? Are you lifting them to greater heights?

When running through Coronado with my newly minted SEAL teammates, we wore sleek running shorts and no shirts. We thought we were cool, but the locals weren't as impressed by our flaunting tough and tanned bodies. They were right, but I didn't care much about it until later when I developed more humility. The uniform of your team, even if a pair of CATCH ME, F*CK ME shorts, will influence one's attitude for better or worse.

In spite of the workout clothes, SEALs exercise harder than

any team I know. Their focus on excellence is relentless and their attention to detail is unprecedented. Having the back of the guy next to you is the core of their value system. Turning a new, challenging action into an SOP (Standard Operating Procedure) was how we succeeded at being uncommon in the SEALs. For instance, after our 7:00 A.M. daily operations meeting, the entire team would go out to the "grinder" to work out together. That began a series of physical and mental actions to forge our bodies and minds. We embraced the suck, and knew we were fire-breathing dragons with a confident mindset and the fittest bodies in the world.

What is your version of becoming a fire-breathing dragon? Hopefully, you're testing your limits now and with time will become the person you have envisioned in your "future me" visualization. Commit to the goal and find a swim buddy, a coach, and a team to train with. Or create one—make it happen!

Once you have a team and routine in place, you won't think twice about it. A quick year from now you WILL be a fire-breathing dragon. Microsoft's co-founder Paul Allen once said: *"Everyone needs a coach. It doesn't matter whether you're a basketball player, a tennis player, a gymnast, or a bridge player."* I've worked to embody this philosophy throughout my life, and I recommend you do too. It's been so satisfying!

CREATE A PLATFORM FOR SUCCESS

Having a professional coach for your physical training is an excellent idea, as well (emotional coaches, aka therapists, are also crucial). A good coach can save you countless hours, prevent bad movement habits and injuries from forming, and keep you motivated and accountable. But before you put money into a coach or trainer, here are some core qualities to look for:

- Experience: You want to find an expert in your field of interest. This shouldn't be too hard nowadays. Reviews are everywhere. And don't save a couple bucks to train with the so-so guy. That would be common and you're uncommon.
- Equanimity: Find someone who sees you and treats you like an equal. A great mentor will hold you accountable, but they can also be counted on both physically to show up and emotionally to have your back.
- Authenticity: An effective mentor is patient but committed, honest, and genuine. They have an instinct for the kind of healthy competition you need on your journey and aren't afraid to push you.
- Allegiance: An effective trainer believes in you.[10]

You want the same kind of traits in your workout partner or team too. A partner or team will ensure you commit deeply, and they will hold you accountable, but you want to make sure they treat you as an equal and believe in your drive and ability. And if you're the team leader, make sure to set milestones and create incentives for the team to reach them. And always be on the lookout for how you can bring others into your movement toward excellence.

Oftentimes, friction in our environment can contribute to the urge to quit the hard work of physical training. For me, going to a dreary, sweaty gym, or hyper-competitive CrossFit Box, are examples of friction. Those are not motivating places for me to train. I like being around positive, collaborative people and I like to train outside in nature as often as possible. My SEALFIT Training Center in Encinitas was 90 percent outdoors (until the city forced us inside, so we moved!). Remove negative friction by choosing, or creating, a positive and collaborative environment in which to train.

And take time to pause, look back, and notice how far you've come after thirty, sixty, or ninety days. Notice how much progress you've made and reward yourself. Take a day off or treat your partner and/or team to something fun.

It is also important to have variety in your training plan as well as athletic goals. Don't hesitate to "shift fire," and adjust your goals if you are starting to get burned out, or they are no longer working for you or the team. This requires weekly or monthly assessments of progress. (Check your tracking journal!) There is simply no straight line to the uncommon success we are striving for. Be okay with that.

As you climb the physical mountain, some may think you are obsessed. They may call you self-absorbed. That's okay. They might have a fixed mindset or are lazy or jealous of your deep commitment to optimal performance and growth. Put your earplugs in and blinders on when this happens. You know now that you must master yourself first before you can serve others well.

At the same time, you really do not want to overdo things. Be balanced and purposeful about your physical training and nutritional fueling. It can become an addiction when you get too attached to a rigid plan or some objective results. It's okay to be deadly serious about developing a new, uncommon lifestyle. But please also be playful, avoid expectation hangovers, and don't be so serious that you compromise your health or become a drag to others. Don't try to be Mr. or Mrs. Perfect. A perfect human and perfect results do not exist. There is only perfect intention with imperfect effort built upon the desire to get better and be more whole. And the road to getting both of those is a windy one!

GAIN TO MAINTAIN

When I moved out of the active-duty navy to become an entrepreneur, I obviously had a strong physical foundation. I just needed to maintain what I had. Easy, right?

Ah, that beautiful word: *maintain.* The imagination conjures up a light run on a sunny day, followed by a beer poolside? Sorry, there is no retirement plan for optimal physical readiness. But holding on to what's already developed is a breeze compared to starting from scratch. If you're already maintaining elite-level fitness, then great work. But if you are like most and have a long way to go, know this: Now that you've committed to mastering your physical mountain, you will get to a point where maintaining your stamina, muscle mass, and flexibility will be simple and feel almost effortless. It will be part of your everyday routine and as important as eating and sleeping. It will be like taking a shower on rising or winding down with a good book before bed. It will become second nature over time.

And all this discipline will lead to enjoyment of hard work combined with a playfulness when you do it. True joy provides the fuel to stay disciplined. My mentor Nakamura was a stern martial arts master, but he was also very spontaneous and playful, with frequent outbursts of hilarity. He was quick to laugh and the first to tell a joke.

You will get there. Stay the course!

EXERCISE 3
Connect for Success

It's okay if you can't see your Uncommon Life clearly. You've already started the how by committing to some simple changes and by envisioning the strong and healthy person you want to become. You can figure out who you need to be, and why, later.

PART 1:
For the third and final exercise in this section, connect to at least one coach, mentor, friend, or team to support you on this journey. This is mandatory! I'd prefer it if you connected in person, but if virtually

is your only option, then find a cyber coach, exercise partner, group, or team who will be there for you on a weekly basis, holding you accountable and vice versa. And create the team if you need to—you're in charge!

PART 2:

Here are the tips again to keep you motivated and focused. Cross out the two additional tips you've added to your routine from Exercise 2 and choose one more from each category to incorporate into your new Uncommon Life!

Physical

- ~~If you're new to exercise, do twenty or more minutes of cardiovascular physical training three to five days a week (or forty minutes if you're already an established exerciser.)~~
- Do some spinal and somatic movement for five minutes every morning.
- Make time for spot drills of squats and push-ups daily.
- Get seven to eight hours of sleep a night.
- Carry fresh water with you and drink it throughout the day.

Mental

- ~~Practice five or more minutes of box breathing daily (building up to twenty minutes).~~
- Read something inspiring for five to twenty minutes (or more) every day.
- Volunteer to do new things or try new things. Say "yes" to helping. It's as simple as that.
- Begin to learn the first most important skill you will need for your new mission.
- Get outside every day to walk, breathe, and clear your head.

Okay, I'm all done preachin'—now go put on your colorful, motivating, and not-at-all-embarrassing workout clothes and get sweating!

BONUS EXERCISE 1
Immersive Learning

If you're on fire and believe your 20X potential has been unleashed, commit to an immersive learning experience on a periodic basis. I shoot for a few a year. This can be an online course (many of which are free) or a weekend retreat. At SEALFIT we offer the SEALFIT Crucible experiences. Or go to a

CrossFit Certification or a yoga retreat. I have over a thousand hours of yoga certification training and months of other meditation, chi gong, self-defense, visualization, and other skill-based training from attending workshops and retreats. Going deep over a period in an immersion training is one of the secrets to accelerating physical and mental growth. These kinds of events or courses will feel like someone put a new battery in your system.

You won't regret it!

MASTERING YOUR PHYSICAL MOUNTAIN *IN REVIEW*

- We learned that more people have a positive energy balance (and hence more obesity) than ever before in history, and it's our job as citizens of Earth to change that and bring the longevity curve back on the rise.
- Our mind wants to come up with excuses of why we don't work out. Moving forward, we must become deaf to the voice in our head that wants to rationalize and keep us common. We all possess transformational superpowers, and once we reach rolling resistance, we will believe we can become the person we've envisioned thirty days, three years, and thirty years from now, for that is the power of momentum.

- We gained strong insight into how exercise is vital to maintaining a healthy brain as we age.
- We learned that cravings and unhealthy eating habits start in our unconscious mind. The stomach wants to eat, and the mind wants to think. We must approach healthy eating from a new angle, from the heart. We must change the way we think about eating.
- Because technology has made us more sedentary, we must move to keep up with the eating habits of our past selves—to keep our pets healthy too. Their lives are also on the line!
- We learned how the power of connection is the biggest force behind success. It's stronger than good genes and all the discipline in the world. We can't do life alone. And we must let go of old ways, and even old friends, to make way for the support system that will run alongside us as we embark up the five mountains.

Congrats, you've made it through Part I. Next up, we are going to learn how to use the body-mind as a whole. We must train it all, not part of it. What did we learn thus far about the brain? That it's 2 percent of our total body mass but uses 20 percent of our fuel. At the end of the day, if your brain is fried, it won't feed your body the correct info to thrive. If it's fried from bad fueling, it's tired and sending those thoughts and emotions to the body. If it's stressed, it's basically going haywire and sending off-the-rails chatter to the body. This is why we will be addressing our thoughts, feelings, and inner and outer awareness for the rest of the book. For the body to be in a state of harmony, the mind must be calm, centered, and focused.

Part II

MASTERING YOUR MENTAL MOUNTAIN

In Part II, we will learn how to start *thinking about our thinking* to reach our 20X potential mind power. And we'll use breathwork, concentration techniques, contemplative journaling, and visualization and imagery practices to launch the journey to mastering our mental mountain.

4

HARNESSING YOUR
20X MIND POWER

magine if Steph Curry had to consciously think about all the steps that go into a three-point shot before each attempt:

Okay, I gotta keep my feet shoulder-width apart, get my shooting foot toe-to-heel in front of the other one, bend my knees, square my hips, straighten my back, get the ball in front of my chest, my shooting elbow in, and my hand under the ball. Now, I need to extend my elbow fast, flick my wrist and fingers to create a back spin rotation on the ball, and keep my eyes on the target after release. Here we go. Eyes on the target!

I'm mentally fatigued just reading that. If we had to depend on our conscious mind every time we shot a basketball, none of us, including Steph Curry, would be worth watching. Yet, all day long we make hundreds of decisions from our conscious mind. And most of the time, these decisions are driven by fear, anxiety, peer pressure, conflicting biases, and unremitting directives. Are those the qualities you look for in a leader? Fear? Weak-mindedness? Bias? Because, if you're not training your mind, you're being led through life by *that guy*.

Sports psychologists are now learning that only 10 percent of success in athletics is achieved in the conscious mind. This means 90 percent is being executed at the unconscious level.[1] Of course, you don't hear commentator Jason Benetti announce: "Curry's unconscious mind just sunk another one!" He'd be out a job if he started talking like that. But make no mistake, at the elite level, that's where most of the work is occurring.

No, I'm not suggesting you need to start training for the NBA to begin your mental training. I harassed you about healthy living in the last section. Now, what I'm saying is to "sink threes in the game of life" with the same kind of ease as the pros, you need to train your mind. This is done primarily through a daily practice of skillful meditation. In that way we can achieve awareness of our thought patterns and begin to control them for positive impact. The more we meditate, the easier it becomes to stay focused, remain positive and free from fear and anxiety, and to make decisions that combine reason with the heart's wisdom.[2] And that's the kind of leader you want in charge of your life, and that the world needs these days.

In Part I, we fueled your motivation and changed your

physical inertia to get you moving toward optimal health and fitness. Now, we're going to change your mental inertia with the ancient mind training of meditation. We will primarily use *breathwork, concentration and mindfulness techniques, contemplative journaling,* and *imagery exercises.* I'm going to teach you how to *win in your mind* to master your mental mountain.

So, let's get busy winning over your mind!

TAME YOUR MONKEY MIND

Most newbies to the Zen bench can't count to ten without their minds starting to wander. And I was no exception.

In 1985 I graduated from Colgate University and headed off to New York City to start my career as an MBA student and budding Certified Public Accountant (CPA). Immediately, I missed the structure that college athletics provided and wondered how I was supposed to maintain my physical and mental sharpness in that intense grind environment. As I considered this, I recalled my college roommate. While I balanced college life with sports and a healthy social life, David trained diligently for his black belt in Shotokan karate. I watched him transform from a lanky, awkward, yet cocky guy into a focused, self-assured warrior. When I graduated, I was older, but I didn't feel my character was any different from when I arrived four years earlier. Hmm.

I wanted to be more complete. I wanted to be more confident and to ease the internal suffering. In other words, I was hungry to be more like David. One evening, as if the universe were answering my request, I wandered past a building and paused under a flag on an awning: WORLD SEIDO KARATE HEADQUARTERS.

Mr. Tadashi Nakamura instantly became a mentor to another desperate seeker. He was the humblest and most integrated individual I had ever met, altering my concept of what a powerful leader looked like. Mr. Nakamura was also a Zen master, and so began my love-hate relationship with the zazen bench (a wooden meditation stool I'd threatened to burn on more than one occasion).

After a few months, I started to notice a shift in my thinking from the Zen meditation. Back in the streets after practice, the air around me felt thicker, as if I were swimming in an energy matrix. I felt connected to my surroundings and more alive during those ten-minute walks home.

And after more than a year of daily Zen practice, I'd developed deep concentration skills and clear metacognition over my thoughts. That meant that I could witness my thinking in "real time," flag negative, distracting chatter, and replace it with a positive internal dialogue. I was also gaining clarity on the flawed nature of my origin stories. Still, I was early in the game of this new form of mental development. I was still unaware that I was both the inmate and the guard in my thought prison, and the vision for my future was still murky, though a sense of being a warrior (and *not* a CPA!) was emerging.

On a new route home from the dojo one evening, a poster

in the window of a navy recruiting office stopped me in my tracks. BE SOMEONE SPECIAL was written across the top of it. Commandos were jumping out of a plane, driving a mini submarine, stalking the enemy. I was captivated and fell into a fantasy, imagining I were them, until my monkey mind took over: *I can't walk away from a secure job. What would my parents say? What would my peers think of me? Where would I be in six years after my commitment was up?* With this negative internal dialogue in charge, I didn't feel very "special." So, I discarded the idea outright.

The next day, against my monkey mind's advice, I asked: *Why not?* I was miserable in my current vocation. I began meditating on this new possibility.

Two long years after standing in front of that poster, I left my "old life" behind—my CPA, MBA, black belt, and even all my belongings—to chase my new most prized possession: the invitation to Navy SEAL training. Like my college roommate David, meditation and a martial arts master helped me tap into uncommon levels of focus, positive energy, and insight. With over a thousand hours on the Zen bench, I had serious new mind power . . . and most important, I had found my purpose. It was November of 1989, and it was just the beginning.

Learning to focus your mind's power is no small task. But it's also no harder than mastering any physical skill— thus all the sports references! It takes years of practice, but all you really have to do is the next practice session. I'm going to reiterate this, so it sinks in: Mastering your mental mountain is achieved through disciplined practice. Period.

THINK ABOUT YOUR THINKING

The first step to winning in your mind is to learn to concentrate so you can focus on "thinking about your thinking." This is a skill called *metacognition*. Developing this skill will not only give you control over the quality of your thoughts, but enable you to move beyond them at will.

According to Dr. Fred Luskin at Stanford University, we have approximately sixty thousand thoughts a day. A whopping 90 percent are repeats from yesterday. (Yes, you read that correctly.) And 80 percent of those thoughts are negative. Is it no wonder you see the world the way you do?

This is a grim reality. Those repetitive, negative thoughts come from our default mode network (DMN).[3] The DMN, referred to as our *ego* by Freud and our *me network* by author and experiential researcher Michael Pollan,[4] is responsible for judgment, self-reflection, tolerance, and magical thinking. And it lights up like a Christmas tree from "likes" on social media sites and negative network news, by the way. It's also the state our minds fall back on when they're not engaged in any focused tasks. Therefore, the common person whose mind is in DMN will ruminate, obsess, fantasize, and freak out in the same thought "fear loop" day in and day out, never taking the time to think about the quality, quantity, or attentional direction of their thought patterns. This will go on for years and decades if left unexamined. That's over fifty thousand useless or negative repeat thoughts a day—most of which undermine body-mind wholeness—ping-ponging around your brain every waking minute.

Do me a favor and "think about what you're thinking about" ten minutes after you set this book down or turn off the audio. Yep, my bet is you are back into the patterns. And tomorrow morning after the blank, beautiful clarity of a new day washes over you as you regain consciousness, pay attention to your thoughts. Do this every morning for the next week. You're going to be bummed that I am right, and that you didn't learn how to control this sooner. But it is never too late!

One second, you're in a complete state of bliss, your mind still and clear. The next, you're stressing about your thesis or work project, reliving a recent fight with your significant other, irked you still haven't finished the DIY project cluttering up the garage, or depressed you still don't fit into those jeans from high school you've been holding on to for the last five or fifteen years.

You sit up to shake off the internal chaos.

And then, in an unfortunate plot twist, you remind yourself to be mad about last night's argument and check your email, which triggers obsessive thinking about work. And you scold yourself for missing the deadline, for the mess in the garage, and for being too big for those damn jeans from high school (which, face it, need to go to Goodwill).

Finally, you rise from bed with troubles in hand, wondering why you slept like hell. Again.

For all you know, you slept great. You just "woke like hell." But give yourself a break. With your DMN thoughts throwing a wet blanket over a potentially perfect day, you never stood a chance.

The DMN racing out of control is one reason people take up drinking, gambling, binge TV series to no end, or spend their weekends swallowed by their favorite social media sites. They're looking for some peace and quiet inside their minds. Those vices capture the mind and turn it right off.

I'm going to show you how to achieve the serenity you're seeking without having to binge *Battlestar Galactica* (an amazing show by the way!) or *The Office* in its entirety for the sixth time next weekend.

Metacognition develops when you learn to concentrate and begin to disengage from those incessant negative thoughts, creating space between them and a new observational capacity, which is often called the *witness*. You develop a sense of being beyond the things you keep thinking about, and you realize that they do not define you. With further development, you will begin to see the underlying beliefs and triggers that created the thought patterns in the first place. And, with dedicated practice, this will enable you to stop the thoughts that aren't serving you, which, if you recall, is about 80 percent of them.

You will not pull this off, however, by dedicating five minutes every other day to Headspace or another popular mindfulness app. I know what you're thinking: *Mark is mean. It's the twenty-first century. Why shouldn't I use one of these cutting-edge apps?* That's like thinking you can become an elite athlete with an online fitness app. There is a steep learning curve to mental development, and we need to get up and over it to the shallow part of the slope. I cannot get you there if you rely on crutches.

What kept me going back to the zazen bench? I felt the changes, and I trusted my teacher, Master Nakamura. But that didn't mean I didn't find it all kinds of frustrating at times. Perhaps because I was miserable in my personal and professional life I felt better after sitting on that darn bench. Also, perhaps I saw it as a challenge and approached sitting on that bench the same way I did swimming or rowing. In fact, I learned that was a mistake and that mental development does not work the same way as physical. More on that later. And perhaps my witness felt the peaceful energy of my mentor and wanted me to have some of that. Regardless, you must trust me when I say that learning to focus the mind and separate yourself from your thoughts will feel like an exercise in futility for a long time. Then, one day, you'll realize the transformation has already occurred, and you'll look back and wonder when that moment was. This is where it starts to get interesting. So, bear with me here, and you'll thank me later.

Once you feel mindfulness in action, you'll be able to examine your thought loops without being triggered or "grabbed" by them. You'll simply observe (or witness) them rising and falling. That's when you can start looking for patterns.

Why would I look for patterns?

. . . Because once you understand your negative thought patterns, you can stop them before they start wrecking your perfectly sunny day. See how it all comes together?

I had to really hone my metacognition for over a year to begin seeing the root cause of my limiting self-concepts. *You're not good enough. . . . You're not good-looking enough. . . . You're not smart enough . . . tough enough. . . .* "I'm not enough" was the tagline in every story I told myself, whether it was from my own perspective or someone else's (a parent, teacher, girlfriend, coworker). "I'm not enough" was grooved into my psyche at a very early age. No, my parents didn't reiterate it during dinnertime. *"Please pass the potatoes, Mark. And don't forget, you'll never amount to anything."* It wasn't that literal. Few things are. But these stories would have been impossible to root out without developing the capacity to think about them with detachment, and then discard them in favor of better options. Our parents or guardians are not evil, not most of them, anyway. What I mean is if we never examine our thoughts and regulate them, we are stuck with our original programming—and that DMN can be very damaging.

The constant exposure to the dialogue and subconscious programming of family and peers creates incessant, omnipresent internal dialogue, imagery, and emotional states that become the never-ending chatter in our mind. I call this our *Background of Obviousness* or *BOO*. This chatter, this BOO, becomes our everyday subconscious chatter and emotional state, which shapes our life story. And most of the time, we're not even aware of it. But, once we examine these thoughts that are running, ruining, and raining all over our sunny days, we will then have the power to challenge them . . . and rewrite them.

Do you accept the premise that you are not your thoughts?

If you answered yes to this question, keep reading. And if you answered no, keep reading too. I love a challenge.

FOCUS YOUR MIND

Carol S. Dweck, PhD, author of *Mindset: The New Psychology of Success,* tells us that we either have a *fixed mindset* or a *growth mindset.*[5] If you haven't developed metacognition and blasted your stories apart, your mindset is fixed. If your mindset is fixed, you crave respect, you demand to be heard, you need to be right. . . . If you have a fixed mindset, you're not listening to the cues around you because you are resistant to change. As long as you're identified with your thoughts, your false origin stories will keep you stuck in Commonland. And you will never achieve your full potential.

Let's not be like that!

The *concentration training* that follows is the first step to help your mind to stabilize and focus in order to unleash the power of metacognition.

But, before we get started, I'm going to get all up in your business. This work of self-transformation is no joke. Most people fail at first attempts because they get trounced by the multitude of obstacles that preexist or arise during the early stages of the process. Here's a list of some of these obstacles. Before you read them, tell yourself they will *not* stop you from developing your 20X mind power. You won't let them!

1. Too busy—not the right time to start training
2. Weak motivation—to climb the ladder at work, find love, get rich

3. Not strong enough direction—no exposure to an authentic teacher

4. The path is too complicated, too difficult to connect with, too esoteric

5. Compromised physical or mental capacity for the training

6. Too easily distracted by sensory attractions—drawn away from the meditation training toward gaming, social media, food, sex, alcohol, drugs, etc.

7. Low on the list of priorities—unfortunate circumstances prevent focused effort, such as living in poverty, fighting cancer, going through a divorce, caring for someone with special needs, working full-time while getting a degree, etc.

8. Boredom—"Meditating sucks."

9. Agnostic, atheist, recovering Catholic, etc.—loss of faith leads to a lack of perseverance

10. Don't know your *why* . . .

Though there are more, those are the top ten excuses I hear most. You will likely confront one or more of them on the path to being uncommon. *For me?* I didn't know my *why,* and I was bored out of my skull. But motivation came easy because of the serious discomfort I was experiencing in my chosen profession. The timing was right, and I had an authentic teacher. I also didn't have to worry about being distracted by the digital world. (The internet wasn't even a thing yet!) I wasn't married with kids or struggling to pay the rent. I had fortunate circumstances. Having said that, if you've gotten this far, it's likely you have *many of* the right conditions to put this training to work for good effect.

There's serious upside to starting your concentration training today. Taking time to meditate every day will also make you more organized and clearer about what to say yes and no to. This magically adds more free time to your busy, overbooked days. It's also an immediate mood enhancer. As you find yourself knuckling down for the first two, ten, twenty, or two hundred sessions, you'll likely catch yourself in a better mood afterward. I've also heard people say, "It just makes life easier." I love that one.

Zen concentration training got me started with a strong foothold on the path to awakening. It was like boot camp for my brain. Thirty-some years back, it was basically divine intervention that I stumbled on a mentor. Today, you have found me ... and other mentors can be surfaced with a simple shout-out to a few friends via text or social media. The wave of mindfulness teachers has been making its way across the Western world for well over two decades now. It's gaining momentum. . . . If you can't find your own Kaicho Nakamura, consider a meditation retreat, authentic yoga training that includes meditation, Transcendental Meditation, or a highly rated online course like Unbeatable Mind. If you prefer to go it alone with me, then you've got this. Easy day.

Concentration boot camp requires that you develop these five basic skills:

- **Focus** your attention on a single thing. What we will use most often is the box breathing pattern.

- **Sustain focus** on the breath (the "thing") by counting the inhale, hold, and exhale, hold for four or five counts. You can also just do inhale five count, pause, then exhale five count, and count the reps. Your goal is to get to ten reps without thinking of anything else.

- **Notice** when you have lost attention control and shifted focus to some DMN thought, emotion, reaction, or other form of self-absorption.

- **Then steer** your attention back to the breath pattern. Doing this is what develops your metacognition over time.

- **Practice this daily to stabilize** your concentration and develop mental power. You will be able to hold your attention on the breathing pattern for longer periods without distraction and notice quicker if/when you get distracted by your DMN monkey mind.

EXERCISE 4
Concentration Training

Let's do five or more minutes of box breathing.

We focus on the breath and the counting to draw attention to the task and reduce the amount of thoughts ping-ponging around our brain. Remember: the nose is for breathing, not the mouth.

Some other concentration tools you may experiment with include:

- External attention meditations such as focusing on a lit candle or any other object. Do your best to breathe evenly, inhaling and exhaling through your nose, and keep your mind clear as you focus your gaze on that object.
- Sound meditation: using a simple mantra, such as "humm" (on inhale) and "so" on exhale, or simply "om," on both is a great way to focus. Also, I like to use short "power statements" that have the additional effect of training positive internal dialogue. My favorites are: "feeling good, looking good, oughta be in Hollywood," and "day by day, in every way, stronger and better, hooyah-he."
- Listening meditation: sitting outside in nature, listening to the sounds around you, works great too.

Congrats. You're on your way to developing metacognition through breathwork and concentration techniques that focus the mind to quiet your DMN— your monkey mind.

Nice work!

In the next chapter, we'll narrow in on our archetypes, an additional tool to keep us on track. We'll learn how to stop the negative thought patterns in our mind to rewrite those stories that create resistance in our lives. And we'll use contemplative journaling to answer the all-important question: *Who am I, really?*

This will start to uncover your *why*.

5

YOUR FUTURE IS NOW

Two monks were traveling together when they came to a river with a strong current. They spotted a young woman waiting, unable to cross alone. Despite the sacred vow they'd taken not to touch women, the older monk picked her up, crossed the river successfully, and set her down on the other side. The younger monk was aghast but kept it to himself. An hour passed, then two hours, then three, until he could no longer take it. "Why did you carry that woman when we took a vow as monks not to touch women?" he asked, agitated.

The older monk replied, "I set her down hours ago by the side of the river. Why are you still carrying her?"[1]

We have a natural tendency to dwell on the past. This interferes with living in the present. I'm not just referring to the deep past, when we think back regretfully on "the one that got away" or the job opportunity we passed up because we were afraid to relocate. I'm talking about ruminating on events from the recent past. Most of us do this obsessively. We do this with near-future events too. In fact, an untrained mind toggles pretty evenly between the discussion that could have gone better earlier that morning at work and the doctor's appointment the following day, not noticing the roses along the way (never mind stopping to smell them). We are still carrying the girl long after we've set her down safely on the other side of the riverbank. (I use the pronoun "we" in a general way here because "you" are putting a stop to all this nonsense.)

There's a reason I set everyone up to master their physical mountain before tackling their mental mountain. Though starting a regular workout routine combined with healthy eating habits may seem daunting, it's easier than embarking on a disciplined meditative practice. It is also imperative because a body that is unhealthy or out of whack is a big distraction. Meditation needs a healthy body as a foundation, which is why most people fail at meditation. Another reason for failure is that, unlike physical training, there is no external evidence that it is working. Those who exercise regularly and maintain healthy diets look better than those who don't. But meditators don't suddenly lose weight and gain muscle mass. If you lined up headshots of me before I ever started meditating, my head is not going to be a few pounds heavier in a year. There is no obvious tell to indicate: *Yeah, the guy on the right is a meditator. Just look at the size of that brain!* There's no physical proof—none that the naked eye can see. But daily meditative practice transforms you and makes you much physically healthier. It just happens at the cellular and energetic levels.

How does it work?

I'm glad you asked! The brain possesses the capacity for neuroplasticity. This means it's capable of reorganizing and creating new pathways and connections. Those add up to more intelligence. Axons can grow new nerve endings, and neural pathways can be created. This happens through the simple act of engaging them. Neurons can be stimulated in one part of the brain to pick up the slack for another, in the case of injury. Or they can be sparked to grow by learning new things, such as a language, a musical instrument, the tango—by reading this book—or from meeting someone new. We also stimulate our neural pathways by exercising them through meditative practices in the same way we increase our upper body strength with push-ups.[2]

Gray matter is positively affected by meditation, increasing the volume, density, and gyrification in the areas of the brain associated with self-awareness, emotion regulation, cognition, and even aging.[3] Aging—wow, right? This growth amps up our self-control, willpower, motivation, and the ability to focus. Meditation fires up the attentional parts of our brain and turns the dial down on the default mode network, which is, again, responsible for self-referential processing and mind-wandering (mainly negative chatter about past and future events we can't control).

What I'm saying is this simple truth: Meditation makes our brains more effective and efficient, and it makes our minds clear and more expansive. This all allows us to move beyond the limiting ego stories that trap us in weak thinking. We must win the battle over our monkey mind and fear-based conditioning. When we do we have total freedom from fear, limitation, and regret. That sounds nice, right? This joyful and clear state of mind is not reserved for monks or enlightened beings. It is your birthright, and I consider it imperative to us thriving as humans.

Understanding what makes you unique and what motivates you is essential to daily meditative practice and to mastering your five mountains. Knowing your *why* will assist in diffusing all the repetitive, ruminative, and negative thoughts and steer your focus back to the now.

The practice of meditation is built upon your daily box breathing practice. So, assuming you are doing it, you have already started the crucial discipline of a daily practice. Your only job, and this is critical, is to KEEP DOING IT!

Now, we will work to uncover your *why* and climb further up the mental mountain.

WHAT IS YOUR WHY?

Not everyone believes that we have a unique purpose in life. Guess what? Those people have not done this work. Obviously, I do believe we all have a unique purpose. My own experience is proof enough for me, but I've also had thousands of clients from all walks of life align with their unique purpose and take off like a bat out of hell in their new, destined directions.

I propose that having a purpose is a primal urge. It's in our DNA, or our soul's calling. Buddhists and yogis call it your *svadharma,* which is your own right or duty, your role in the cosmic order or in the grand scheme.[4] This is not the same as going after a specific job or career. I consider it to be an archetypal energy . . . the way you came into this world that makes you uniquely qualified and compelled to serve in a certain way. You don't have to believe in karma, past lives, or God to feel this. But you can see it in the patterns of your thinking and why you made certain decisions in your life. Things that you love, your passions, the people you gravitate toward—you'll find your stories, leading to insight on how you should and shouldn't be, living in these patterns. You can also uncover it in meditation by learning to listen to your heart's "inner voice." That is how I heard my archetypal urge to be a warrior, and it led me from being a CPA into the SEAL teams.

Your purpose is not going to be one of those things you use as an identifier: such as "I am a doctor, a parent, a teenager, an elite runner, a tattoo artist, a snowboarder, a neat freak, or a night owl." When I said to myself, "I'm a Navy SEAL officer," I was not stating my why, or purpose. That was simply a role I was filling that was in alignment with my purpose of being a warrior and leader. Your purpose is a way of being, a way of serving, but it is not a job or career path. It does point the way though.

The archetypal roles conceived by world-renowned Swiss psychiatrist Carl Jung identify what we, as individuals, seek to realize in this lifetime. Some people are healers, some are warriors, others are jokers, leaders, teachers, explorers.[5] We usually have more than one archetype, though one of the archetypal energies will be dominant, such as: social entrepreneur, elite warrior, professor of truth, colonizer of space, servant to the poor, protector of humanity, healer of broken people, advocate for Mother Earth, honest politician, trusted diplomat, creative genius, etc.

Find your archetypal energy, fueled by your unique passions, skills, and principles, and you'll be on your way to the Uncommon Life. If you know it now, write it down!

The purpose of my life is to serve as a _____

_____.

As I mentioned, when I settled into this inquiry in my meditation practice, what came up was *warrior*. The first iteration was as a warrior-athlete and then warrior-leader. Later it became warrior-strategist and warrior-teacher. When I had that revelation, I sought to align my profession with that newfound archetypal purpose. But I didn't immediately figure out it was going to be the SEALs. In fact, I was not thinking about the military at all. So, if you think you are a warrior also, that doesn't have to lead to a career in the military. You can be a warrior-scholar, -athlete, -leader, or any of the archetypes and find a way to build a profession around your unique skills, passions, and principles.

Defining yourself in archetypal energy, such as a "warrior-leader," focuses you on "being" instead of "doing," which gives you room to grow and expand. This can change as you evolve (otherwise, you'd be pigeonholing yourself). A Navy SEAL admiral would not have been something I was becoming, my archetype. That would have been a tactical career goal, and it would have inhibited the new archetypal energy of the teacher that was emergent in me from surfacing. I would have spent all my time thinking about, and working on, becoming an admiral, serving in that capacity, instead of exploring the new energy of the author and teacher. I would never have written my books or developed my training programs. Who knows what else would have been different? That is why I feel this issue is so darn important, and I'm hammering it home.

I stumbled on an interesting story relating to this point while writing this. Vikramjit Singh, born and raised in Punjab, India, started out in a traditional career path, studying engineering at the Manipal Institute of Technology. He then went on to work as an associate software engineer in Bangalore. But, even when he was getting his degree, Singh spent most of his free time writing and performing in different theatres and literary clubs. After college, though effective in his field, he spent his days with that faint ache in his heart, knowing he was not aligned with his purpose. So, he went from being an engineer to a copywriter for a stint. That got him on the writing track. But then, his destiny was realized when he made the leap and became a stand-up comedian. *"Engineering was reduced to an extra-curricular activity. So that just put me on a course that I kept following organically—through various jobs, until I finally decided to write and perform for a living."* Using YouTube as a vehicle to reach a bigger audience, he's gaining traction on the world stage.[6]

Singh was living as a creator but was unfulfilled, so he

shifted closer to his true archetype, taking on the role of a communicator. Changing the inertia of his direction led him to his niche as a joker. Is this his final destiny? I doubt it. I'll be interested to see what Singh is doing ten years from now. I know he'll take direction from his whole mind, that much seems obvious.

Just imagine what you—*and the world*—will miss out on if you don't align with your purpose.

Your professional options will be determined by how your purpose, passions, and principles align with your unique skills, and by what the world needs. Once I identified my purpose after hundreds of hours on the meditation bench, I continued to work at my current job but shifted my focus and training to the new path. I knew where I needed to point my compass. My visualization, meditation, contemplation, and insight training shifted to my new, emerging, future self.

It is important to reiterate that as you evolve, so will your archetypal purpose. When I first figured this out in my early twenties, I was living the role of the merchant but was not inspired. My insight pointed to the warrior and leader. Then, in my thirties, as I was fulfilling the role of the warrior and leader, I felt the scholar emerge. So, I went to the University of San Diego to get my PhD in Leadership (I later finished it at Pepperdine after getting distracted by the Iraq War). I became an adjunct professor as well. Then, wanting to actually develop leaders rather than teach leadership in a sterile classroom, I launched SEALFIT and Unbeatable Mind. I later taught on stages and through my books and podcast.

The archetypal roles evolved as I did. The warrior was always present, but later on it took on a supporting role. I'm currently a teacher of warriors and leaders. But, as I look ahead, I see a warrior-monk emerging. The warrior archetype threads throughout my life, dominant in my earlier years, now giving way to the softer energy of spiritual development. It is crucial to align your career with your archetypal energy to find absolute fulfillment and continue to serve most powerfully.

Don't panic if you don't know your why and calling. I'm not suggesting you spend years career hopping to find it. I'm saying that sitting in meditation will bring that clarity of your why and how you can best serve humanity.

As this practice unfolded for me, I was compelled to ask questions not about what I should or could do, but about how I should be. I experienced imagery and feelings about the "being me" desperate to emerge. When my Zen sessions ended and I reentered my daily life as a CPA, I would experience mild suffering from being out of alignment with the new vision of how I should be: a warrior. I could see a big gap between the person I sensed in my meditation and the person who showed up at work every day.

Sticking with the practice stoked my need to rectify this misalignment. I felt an urgency to take a stand, one that put me in conflict with my earlier choices. This is a universal, perennial struggle, and one that I embodied. One that Singh had clearly embodied. One that you can embody now if you feel out of alignment (and my experience is that most people do feel out of alignment). I believe it is utterly imperative to find your calling . . . and take a stand to fulfill it or suffer life with that faint ache in your heart and that nagging feeling in your guts. Henry David Thoreau said that most people lead lives of quiet desperation. That is common . . . but that is not you.

Meditation came into my life when I was just twenty-one. I might have been one of those guys dealing with a midlife crisis right now were it not for that "sign."

LIKES AND DISLIKES

By year two of meditation, I began to *contemplate* what was wrong with my choices, with inquiries such as: *Why am I not happier? What is it about this life that isn't working? What thoughts are limiting me?* But I couldn't identify a positive path forward. It's not like I suddenly heard from deep down: *Mark, you're supposed to be a Navy SEAL officer. Get after it.* No, first I had to identify what, specifically, was wrong with my current path. When I started getting answers, I was more aware of the things that needed changing, which was cool. But I didn't know what I was going to change them to, which wasn't so cool.

At least I'd begun to see why I was shut down emotionally, and why I drowned my suffering with beer and hard physical training in futile attempts to feel more alive. But with no clear answers, I decided to make a **list** of all the things that I disliked and didn't want to see in my life. And then I made another list of the things I loved about living.

The Dislikes List included . . . a lot:

I don't like putting a suit on every day.

I don't enjoy playing the rat race game.

I don't like the profession I'm in.

I don't like crunching numbers (I'm not great at math or accounting).

I don't care for New York City, except for my martial arts training.

I don't connect with the people I'm around most of the day.

I don't like feeling that I have to sneak away from work to exercise.

I don't like living in a concrete jungle, disconnected from nature.

I don't like the idea of being inside every day, doing the same thing over and over.

I don't like having a cubicle as an office.

I don't like the idea of money and prestige as my only rewards for work.

I'm turned off by the ego around how much one makes as a measure of their life.

There were scads of things that I didn't care for, or connect with, in my everyday world. . . . Yet, there I was, immersed in them all. Eek. Once my list of negatives was right there in front of me, I could starkly see the gap between my reality and my desires. Next, I compiled a list of my likes and passions. The Likes List included:

I love being physically fit.

I love adventure.

I love a good challenge.

I enjoy growth.

I crave constant improvement.

I love reading.

I love traveling.

I love the outdoors and nature.

I like silence. In fact, I'm beginning to really enjoy spending time in silence.

When I was in the Adirondacks as a kid, I was at my most happy being alone in the wilderness.

In the city, the silence of Zen practice was a substitute for the tranquility I'd felt in nature. This line of contemplation uncovered what I was truly passionate about and led to defining what I valued most. When I studied both lists with an open mind, I was able to see things objectively and from a place of detachment. And I asked:

Is what I'm doing now in alignment with the things that I am passionate about and value most?

Of course, the answer was a big, fat, from the top of my

lungs *NO!* I was in alignment with what I didn't like and didn't value. The stories I'd been telling myself drove me to make choices that made life miserable. Understanding that truth was groundbreaking. It allowed me to seek answers to my dilemma through this series of questions:

How did I get myself onto this path? (Why did I make the decisions I made that led me here?)

What have I done well? (What am I good at?)

What are the top three activities I love to do?

What are my top three principles I want to guide my behavior as I make a stand?

What should (can) I do right now to align with my desires?

If this path is wrong, what path is right? (Do I know my calling?)

If I do know my calling, how can I move toward that path now?

It would take me about nine more months for this process to unfold until, finally, I'd have a much clearer picture of what I stood for. And what I didn't. And what I "could do now" to get onto the right path. This story of how I went from a CPA to the SEALs personifies the profound effect changing your inertia of direction can have on your life course.

Are you ready to find out what you stand for?

Here we go!

EXERCISE 5
The Lists

Knowing what you're passionate about helps define your calling or purpose. Let's take a deep look at your likes, dislikes, and what you value (your guiding principles) to narrow this down. This is going to be easy-peasy. You have all my answers as a cheat sheet!

You're going to create a Likes List and a Dislikes List in your journal and then contemplate the results.

Find a comfortable place and sit down.

Get still with five minutes of box breathing, and let all external distractions go. Now, let's start with your Dislikes List, which I like to do first, as our higher-thinking brains love to "default" to a negative state. Don't forget you can refer to my list, and here are some prompts to help too.

I don't like . . .
I don't enjoy . . .
I don't care for . . .
I don't connect with . . .
I'm turned off by . . .
I struggle with . . .

Write your thoughts down, as many as come to mind.

Now, take a short break before you shift gears and create your Likes List. Here are some prompts to assist you:

I like . . .
I enjoy . . .
I love . . .
I crave . . .
I'm passionate about . . .

You will have deeper insights as you work with this over the course of a few days—and the following ninety days. The next step in this exercise is to get into a deep, relaxed state, and just look at your two lists with a non-judging mind. Look for the obvious patterns. Where do they line up? Where are they out of synch? Ask yourself:

Is what I'm doing now in alignment with the things I'm passionate about and value most?

Your answers will vary. But if you're way out of alignment, it's because you were working with bad information, your story was wrong, and you didn't know your *why* or how to do this work. Or, maybe, you knew you were out of whack but haven't found the courage to change until now. Your Likes List represents your most important passions and principles. These will point toward your archetype and overarching purpose in life. Make note of how these "likes" could play out in your life when you move toward them.

Now it's time to uncover your purpose, which is in alignment with your passions and principles. Answer these questions:

How did I get myself onto this path? (Why did I make the decisions I made that led me here?)
What have I done well? (What am I good at?)
What are the top three activities I love to do?
What are my top three principles I want to guide my behavior as I make a stand?
What should (can) I do right now to align with my desires?
If this path is wrong, what path is right? (Do I know my calling?)
If I do know my calling, how can I move toward that path now?

A life lived on purpose that's in alignment with your principles and fueled by passion is the goal. It will be amazing. Do you know, based on the work we just did, what your archetype is? List as many possibilities as you need to and, as we move through the book, we can narrow it down.

1. _____

   _____

2. _____

   _____

3. _____

   _____

Thanks to breathwork and concentration exercises, we are developing your metacognition. Thanks to contemplative journaling, which has uncovered your likes and dislikes, you know who you are at your core, what you stand for, and you're ready to fight for your *why*.

Through daily meditative practice, you're quieting your monkey mind and achieving pure awareness of your thoughts, which creates positivity and self-control. The practice to become the person you envision has begun. You can't wing your destiny any longer!

In the next chapter, we're going to set the conditions to win in your mind so that the future comes to you as you become the person worthy of that future.

6

ENVISION YOUR DESTINY

Construction began on Sagrada Familia basilica in 1909. It is the tallest church in all of Europe, and considered a masterpiece. Thanks to computers, it finally has a completion date in 2026, over one hundred years later. Architect Antoni Gaudí envisioned this work of art before the capability to complete it was even invented.

That's uncommon.

Leonardo da Vinci conceived a flying machine based on birds in flight four hundred years before the Wright Brothers successfully built one with a gasoline-powered internal combustion engine. SpaceX CEO Elon Musk imagines a colony on Mars living inside glass domes, with a long-term plan for generating propellant for the rocket flights using sustainable energy.[1] But Musk admits he won't likely be alive to become a resident of the community. Still, that probability hasn't stopped this uncommon visionary.

If you have dreams of something that has yet to exist

in this world, don't let that stop you from working hard to become the next architect, or artist, or scientist to make your imaginings a reality. Don't limit the vision you have for your future. Gaudí, da Vinci, and Musk all envisioned their dreams with minute detail, as has been evidenced by architectural drawings, brush and ink illustrations, and spacecraft designs. With visions that clear, no wonder they've transformed the world and made the history books. We're going to learn how to do this, too, to open the door to your dreams.

If you've read this far, you likely already believe that your thoughts influence your mood and physical well-being, and you'd like to have more control over them. Further, you believe meditation techniques will help you achieve this goal. But, did you know that this ability to direct your thoughts to manifest a future event is the single most powerful tool that you possess?

It is.

Visualization and other imagery exercises were not much spoken of when I first envisioned being a SEAL in the mideighties. My experiences, and the experiences of great sports legends who have utilized imagery for great success, are changing that. I learned that for imagery to be the potent force that I claim it to be, it must become an emotionally evocative, whole, body-mind practice. What this means is when you see an event clearly in your mind, you will also feel it intensely throughout your physical body. Then you can begin to "know" it intimately as an aspect of your being, a "future self" experience being experienced in the now moment in your mind's eye. It is also important to note that what we practice in our mind at this level of intensity must be in alignment with your heart's desires. Otherwise, your ego will get involved and you may get something you don't need, or worse, regret. So, let's be careful about what we put these skills to work on. Imagery has been used to manipulate humanity for countless years, and you don't want to play that game. In fact, we are seeking total freedom from any manipulation or being under the control of any person or entity. We use these skills to find and fulfill our purpose, and for good. Period.

Just as you visualized what your ideal fit and healthy body would look like in the physical mountain, you will use imagery work to achieve mental mountain mastery, to envision your ideal future self, and to practice your one-thing mission. We will use the crawl-walk-run approach to train this amazing skill.

Think about a simple event, such as hanging out on a warm beach with your best friend on a well-earned vacation. Even that short and sweet snapshot—two friends on the beach—evokes a physical, emotional, and sensory reaction. You created a reality for your body-mind: your shoulders likely relaxed, you got a warm feeling in your heart, and a small smile may have even formed on your face. Some of you may have felt a warm ocean breeze and smelled the salty air. This happens because our physical body is a projection of the mind, so will experience at a physical level what the mind dwells on with potent imagery. If you imagine fearful things all the time, your body will experience anxiety and illness. If you imagine beautiful things, your body will be relaxed, stress free, and calm. Your body expresses the mind's reality.

Let me say this again: our body lives in the state our mind tells it to. Got it? Learning this was a watershed moment in my life. I became acutely aware of my thoughts and the imagery they evoked . . . and began to curate their quality to be more positive, forgiving, and beautiful. My body has been in perfect health and fitness ever since.

Okay, now imagine the power of reinforcing your mind's desire by taking action daily toward becoming über-healthy and fit, *and* also making your purpose-fueled vision a reality. Wow, right? BTW, thinking obsessively about a future not based upon your heart's calling (what I just referred to as your purpose-fueled vision) is fantasizing, and more often than not, your DMN will lead you down the wrong road.

To manifest your purpose-fueled destiny, any and all disempowering stories holding you back will need to be eradicated and replaced by new empowering stories. To do this, we will start developing a new internal dialogue, accompanied with imagery and emotions that support your emergent dream. If you want to influence a billion people and become a billionaire, then you need to think and be someone worthy of that level of leadership and service. It is completely doable because you get to decide how to construct "your" world. And your world is the only world there really is for you. So, you need to begin to see, feel, and embody this new figure, experience the emotions of being a world-renowned leader or a billionaire. When your future memories (recall I stated that an imagined future is a memory of a future yet to happen) and emotions line up with your current thoughts, words, and emotions, then stunning results will follow.

"MENTAL" PRACTICE MAKES PERFECT

Most, if not all, elite athletes use visualization and imagery techniques regularly. Olympic swimmer Michael Phelps visualizes his events before *and* after each race. He has won twenty-five gold medals. The Navy SEALs visualize their missions before they jump into the dark night to execute them, and they have a 95 percent success rate. This skill is even more powerful when done with a whole team. At my company we are teaching corporate teams to visualize their future and mission outcomes together, and they are finding they are navigating this crazy world with more success and confidence.

Mental practice will get you as close to perfect as you'll ever come—but don't mistake perfect visualizations for perfection in the pool or on the field or at the conference (or in the jungle). You and your teams are not likely to be perfect at anything, ever. When you practice anything in the real world, be it sports, musical instruments, surgery, or what have you, your skills improve but rarely reach perfection. When you practice those same skills in your mind, however, you get to control all the variables, especially the outcome. That means it is *perfect practice* that leads to optimal results for *that day and time of the performance*. Decades of studies have shown that mental repetition, with perfect form, yields better results than physical practicing alone.

In an interesting experiment at the University of Chicago back in the 1950s, Dr. Biasiotto wanted to test the power of visualization to improve athletic skills. He took ninety college students and had them practice free throws for an afternoon, recording their individual stats. Then, he split them into three groups. The first group practiced shooting for an hour every day. The second group merely visualized shooting free throws every day. The third group was a control group that did nothing. After thirty days, Dr. Biasiotto brought everyone back in and had them shoot, recording their stats. The group that practiced one hour daily improved by 20 percent collectively. The visualization group improved 19 percent—without ever touching a basketball! The control group showed no improvement at all. Here's the biggest catch: none of these students had ever shot a basketball prior to his study.[2] Imagine getting better at a skill you never physically practiced?

How is that possible?

Success starts with winning in the mind. If you're trying to develop top athletic skills, it starts in the mind. You see yourself doing it, which creates self-belief. Then, you begin the task of practicing the activity to develop the basic skills, and you grow from there. This happens naturally. We don't try out for a team or pick up an instrument or any new hobby without imagining ourselves doing it. Most of the time we're not conscious, however, that we're doing this. We're not focused on the mental part of the exercise, so it goes by the wayside as soon as we start to work to master the physical skill.

But remember: The body-mind doesn't discriminate between visualizing and performing . . . *because our body lives in the state our mind tells it to.* The same neural pathways that arise from learning something new or having a new experience develop when we visualize performing a new skill, having a new experience, or achieving a new goal. The body might not be chasing a ball around a court and breaking out in a sweat, but the brain, as Dr. Biasiotto's study proved, is being trained to perform the tedious skill of shooting, nonetheless. This is the body-mind connection.[3]

When I was at Colgate University, my swim coach had me visualize my two-hundred-meter breaststroke race with a stopwatch. It was a real challenge to hold my concentration for that long. It took me several months before I could finish the entire eight lengths and press stop on the watch. When I was finally able to do it, the time that I swam mentally was about three seconds faster than my fastest actual swim time. It doesn't sound like much, but for competitive swimming, that is a very long time! I never realized that time in that school year, and the following fall semester I went to London for an economics semester abroad. When I returned to school the following spring, I ran into my coach, who invited me to jump in the water for the team's final meet. I hadn't been in a pool for close to a year, yet as I jumped off the blocks into the water, I had this feeling that I had swum this race before. I was relaxed (which is another key to peak performance that is enhanced with mental training) and finished the event three seconds faster than my fastest time! That was a powerful anchor telling me that effective, sustained visualization practice is an extraordinarily powerful tool.

Bottom line: If you want to be uncommon and serve in a unique way, you must see what you desire, and then practice it in your mind. Your desired future depends on this.

You are today the person you saw five years ago doing the things you're now doing. You're the countless small choices you have made because of that vision. Do you want that same person to show up for the next five years? If not, you've got to imagine something different. Change your story to change your choices, change your imagery to change your life.

You won't likely see massive results at first. Most of my students have trouble holding their concentration when they start. Others can't see anything in their mind's eye. These skills are cultivated through daily practice.

Most of us are strong in rational and linear thinking skills. The world is mostly left brained, which is our logical side. So, if you have a predisposition for imaginative thought, then consider yourself lucky. That type of thinking will be crucial in the future.

Regardless of your current skill base, practice is the only way to hone your visual mind.

SPEAK TO YOURSELF KINDLY

It's not enough to visualize something to truly believe it. Our biases, our subconscious programming, our BOO can interfere with this process. You may have a natural negative disposition, unmanaged anxiety, or a feeling of inadequacy. Your self-talk, reactionary emotions, and lack of self-belief prevent your imagery from forming a strong foundation. Any dissonance between thoughts, emotions, beliefs, and imagery will put out conflicting signals that cancel each other out. We practice daily concentration skills, and we journal to overcome this. But here's another technique to add to your arsenal. . . .

Visualizing a different future starts with initiating new internal dialogue.

Back in the eighties, before I met Kaicho Nakamura or knew about visualization or any of this stuff, I happened upon a motivational tape. (Yes, it was a cassette I had to listen to on a tape recorder!) It was by author and motivational speaker Brian Tracy.[4] At the time, any imagery I did have was colored by a small-town upbringing and challenging family dynamics, and my story was absent of any empowering visions for my future.

I learned a few important things from this audiobook, but one simple tool stood out. Tracy suggested practicing a positive mantra to change your relationship with the most important person in your life . . . you! His advice was to simply say this over and over: "I like myself. I like myself. I like myself." I started to do this every morning on rising. I know it sounds kind of silly, but it had a powerful effect. Several months later, I started to see myself a little differently. This daily mantra was pushing out old emotions, and I was feeling better about myself. It was lifting me up. Ironically, it is still with me to this day, showing up whenever my brain regains consciousness every morning!

Tracy didn't suggest imagery to rewrite my old story. He basically said: "*Hey, give this a try. It helps to talk to yourself kindly.*" If you struggle with self-esteem as I did, and many people do, then I recommend you start doing this today.

Armed with growing self-confidence from this simple technique, along with Zen meditation training, which started a year or so later, my mental development really took off. After practicing Zen for about six months, I began to get a clearer sense of how my stories had limited me. I started to see the potential for someone different emerging—someone compassionate, competent, and courageous—so I decided to trust that new intuition and run with it. My mantra evolved and became: "I am a warrior and a leader, and I like myself." I want you to know this process of speaking a new reality internally was difficult at first because the old storyteller in me kept interrupting! But I stuck with it. . . .

When I finally got to the SEALs, I wanted to continue the power of mantra, so I created a new one: "I'm looking good, feeling good, oughta be in Hollywood." The constant repetition of a mantra had a powerful effect to keep me positive and focused. And I began to really see myself as the kind of guy who was worthy of being in Hollywood. Keep in mind, I knew nothing of Hollywood, and I wasn't shooting for that as a career, but it activated in my body-mind powerful imagery and emotional states that propelled me through the intense challenges of Basic Underwater Demolition/SEALs training.

If you've ever told yourself that you're, for example, a klutz over and over and continue to be klutzy, mix it up. Decide you have the power, grace, and balance of a member of the Shaolin monks. Test that new mantra with imagery for a few months and get back to me. You can change any story by telling yourself the opposite, even if you don't believe what you're crooning.

It took several months of faithful practice of Mr. Tracy's recommendation before I really started to like myself. I'm glad I trusted him and did that work, and hope that you'll decide to give positive, emotionally charged internal dialogue a try.

IMAGINE YOUR IDEAL FUTURE

Fantasy is fueled by unexamined desire stirred up by your ego's DMN. Visualization is fueled by examined desire flowing from your witness, which is your highest self. You may fantasize about something you think you wish for, but it is not something you need, and it's not aligned with your purpose. Oftentimes, it's not possible or it's plain outlandish. People fantasize about winning the lottery, going back in time and buying Bitcoin at twenty cents, or reconnecting with an old boyfriend or girlfriend. I've had those fantasies myself—they're a waste of time. Now that you're becoming more aware of your thoughts, you'll be able to stop those when they start, and redirect.

Visualization is the practice of imagining a newly defined "ideal future" that you deeply desire. It's also a reimagining of your past in a way that is productive and beneficial to your present and future. It's also another way to practice an emergent skill you're developing or refining to a higher level. Visualization will help you master that skill faster.

Imagine my ideal future? But I have no idea what that could look like. . . .

That was the case with me before the SEALs and with most audacious things I have leaned into—no worries!

You just need some imagery to seed your visualization. Back in the early days, my imagination was well trained through fantasizing being anywhere else besides where I was. So, when I began to envision myself as a SEAL, imagery itself was not hard for me. But to imagine something radically new and different to achieve a specific future result was new to me. It is important to have some context and reference imagery to anchor your practice. This is much easier now with all the TV and other imagery about almost anything you want. Back in the eighties, practically nothing public was available about the SEALs except for a simple recruiting video. It had imagery of real trainees doing cool things. I played it over twenty times to download the imagery into my brain. Then I inserted myself into that imagery to turn it into a practice visualization. I visualized myself going through this training every morning after my run. After several months of this practice, I felt myself gaining confidence. At around nine months of the practice, I had a shift in my consciousness with a sudden "knowingness" that I would be a Navy SEAL, that it was my destiny. It did not, however, turn me into a sharp-shooter or magically give me leadership skills. Those skills came with on-the-job training.

Some other self-help authors have recommended creating a *vision board* to represent your dream. That's a good first step to help get clear on the imagery for your future goals. But it is not enough. You must relentlessly practice the future vision in your mind every day. Another helpful approach is to look at successful people doing what you want to do and imagine being just like them. This is why the right mentors can be so powerful, as this can happen through transference. I imagined myself being like Nakamura, and now I am. First you will want to write out your vision and read it before sitting down to visualize it. That helped me immensely. Eventually, the new memory of the desired future will solidify in your mind and draw you toward it like a magnet. That's when I started adding finer details, using all the senses.

Daily visualization practice not only builds confidence, but it also strengthens other aspects of your mind. You'll be able to hold your concentration longer. You'll see your thoughts in action more clearly. You'll become a better listener without even trying. Your ability to communicate honestly and compassionately will reach new heights. These skills provide even more courage to go after things you once thought unreasonable.

Visualization practice evolves as you evolve.

To achieve my current dream, I have had to step up my

game once again and visualize the person I need to be for it to happen. I'm not just going to rest on my laurels as a former Navy SEAL, author, or whatever. Just like you're doing now, I am reinventing myself once again, and that will happen over and over. We have to develop the muscle to reinvent ourselves constantly, and it is done with new self-talk, imagery, and feelings about the desired future to make it happen.

It's exciting, knowing we can reinvent ourselves at will.

VISUALIZATION PRACTICE #1

Your brain dedicates different areas for visual, emotional, and verbal expression. We say we're *remembering* when we look back and *visualizing* when we look forward. In both cases, we can attach visual aids, emotions, and verbal triggers to these images—and we can alter our *memories* and our *visions* to change how we feel about them, using our whole mind to change how we think at the unconscious level.

Let's start our practice by bringing this basic past experience into the present:

Visualize a lemon in your hand.
Look at it.
Hold it.
Feel it.
It's roundish.

It's yellow with little indentations.

Now cut it in half.

Bring it to your mouth.

Squeeze it into your mouth.

What happens?

Did you pucker?

Can you taste the sourness of the lemon?

Can you see the lemon in your hand?

What dialogue came up?

What other imagery appeared?

What emotions arose?

This is a good practice to start visualizing—by recalling something simple and familiar that you're not necessarily attached to emotionally but uses some of the senses.

VISUALIZATION PRACTICE #2

In your mind's eye pick up a delicious, red apple.

Look at it.

Turn it around in your hand.

You notice a wormhole.

As you look at it, a cartoon worm pops out.

It's wearing a top hat and eyeglasses. It has a mustache and it's smoking a cigar.

This worm winks at you and says, *"Howdie, what's shakin'?"*

This is an example of visualizing something you've never experienced. But don't be mistaken, this is fantasy, as this could never happen. This is a ridiculous fantasy but imagine if you wasted precious time thinking about this top-hat-wearing, cigar-smoking, talking worm. Does that sound healthy? Exactly. Let's start replacing those fantasies with something that serves you.

VISUALIZATION PRACTICE #3

You're swimming in the ocean.

You see a shark fin behind you.

You swim faster.

The shark swims faster.

Every time you increase your speed, the shark swims faster.

The beast, with its mouth agape, is gaining on you.

You can't outswim it.

You turn, seeing his jaws opening wider. . . .

Notice the anxiety that imagery creates. Can you feel the tingling of fear welling up from your gut? Rereading the above scenario will only reinforce the fear, again and again. *Did you reread it?* This kind of visualization, a far-fetched fantasy for most of you, creates a strong, unpleasant emotional sensation in our guts.

This is why you don't want to practice visualizing things you fear or don't want. It will just reinforce those things in your life . . . bringing the feeling of it into your physical body, again and again. Do you visualize fear of failure, rejection, loss, or anything else negative? Whatever your story, whatever you tell yourself, every time you see it in your mind's eye, you're reinforcing it in your neural pathways, and sending that sensation into your body.

EXERCISE 6
Future Me Visualization

Have your journal handy before you begin this exercise.

- Get yourself in a comfortable position . . . sit down with your back straight.
- Do five minutes or more of box breathing to tap into your higher self, your witness.
- Begin the practice of seeing yourself as a person worthy of your 20X self: 20X health, 20X intellect, 20X emotional power, 20X performance. Imagine what you would look like and be like.
- See yourself achieving the things that you will be capable of when you become that version of yourself.
- Visualize yourself as incredibly successful at what

you'd love to do (that's aligned with your purpose, passion, and principles).

It's now time to develop a positive future vision. Take out your journal and answer these questions:

What do you see yourself doing?
Who have you become?
What does it feel like to be that person?
What is better about your life?

See yourself fulfilling the future that's predicted in your vision. Write down your vision if you're so inspired! Collapse this image to the present day. Now, go and practice "today" from the point of view of your ideal future self, as if you are already that person. See yourself deeply focused, hitting your targets, knocking down the obstacles from the perspective of *that* person.

This experience feels a lot different from being chased by a shark, right? The more imagery in your mind about your ideal future, the more you will feel it strongly and believe it in your heart, and the easier it will become to speak it to others. Then, soon enough, it will become real.

See it. Feel it. Believe it. Say it. Do it.

That's uncommon.

MASTERING YOUR MENTAL MOUNTAIN *IN REVIEW*

- We practiced breathwork (box breathing) and concentration techniques to develop metacognition. This will literally make your brain bigger, turning on your control centers and turning down your default mode network, your monkey mind.

- We started contemplative journaling with Likes and Dislikes lists to uncover our *why,* and we narrowed down our archetypal energies so that we can change our inertia of direction to begin living our purpose.

- We learned how the power of visualization can manifest our desired future. By shifting our internal dialogue using positive self-talk (mantras) and by rewriting and controlling our past and future memories, we can enhance and expedite this process.

In Part III: Mastering Your Emotional Mountain, I will help you build the bulletproof plan you're imagining and preparing for in your mind. And I will train you to create laser-like focus and resiliency, through good times and bad, to keep you moving forward on your new trajectory. When the uncommon becomes common to you, you become extraordinary in the eyes of others. And maintaining that will require a whole new level of emotional strength.

Part III

MASTERING YOUR EMOTIONAL MOUNTAIN

- We'll investigate what emotions are, how they link every system in our bodies, and how they affect every experience we have. We'll break down the mind-body (intellectual-emotional) connection to understand why it's imperative we feed courage and starve fear to master our emotional mountain and build resiliency.

- We'll take a close look at our shadow selves, our BOO, and learn how to let go of the origin stories that have been holding us back through a process called *recapitulation*.

- We'll take a deeper look into the emotions of regret and worry to gain insight on how one keeps us in the past, the other in the future, and how both emotions remove us from living in the present.

- Finally, we'll put an end to the everyday emotions that hold us back from becoming uncommon.

7

THE POWER OF EMOTIONS

started my college career majoring in premed, enrolling in English, calculus, biology, and physics the first semester. I really enjoyed physics, but the class was huge, with over a hundred students, and was taught by an Iranian professor who spoke broken English. There was no feedback, no quizzes or homework, just a midterm and a final.

I studied my ass off for the midterm. And I got a 40 percent. I was devastated.

I'd never failed anything in my life. And the concept of resiliency was a distant lesson.

I went to see the freshman dean. It was his first year at Colgate too. He immediately and confidently suggested I wasn't cut out for premed and that I should drop the course. I went to see my professor, and he agreed with the dean.

So, I dropped the course, and that was the end of my premed career.

Deciding I was mentally unequipped for the rigid academics

required for medicine, I shifted to what I deemed an easier major: economics. As that first painful semester of college wound down, I found the courage to approach a premed friend who had joined the same fraternity about his experience with physics.

"Boy, I really torched that midterm," I said to Chris. "I had to drop the class."

"Yeah," he said, "Me too. I got like a twenty on it."

"Huh, what?"

"Yeah, yeah, he had to grade on a curve because everyone failed."

"Well, I got a forty on it."

"Dude, then you had one of the highest grades in the class!"

. . . Well there you go. I learned then not to trust "the experts" all the time. And I also learned that all of life is graded on a curve. The irony is that I would have made a terrible medical professional. I can't stand the sterile environment of the lab or the hospital. So those people actually did a great favor for me by derailing me from a wrong-path decision. The final lesson from this interesting experience is that often the universe will give you what you need, and not what you want.

However, at that time the incident piled onto the inferiority complex I had in my own intellectual ability. Sophomore year, I decided to step up my game and do things differently by modeling two all-star academic guys from my fraternity, Dan and Gary. They had been accepted to a London semester abroad program at the London School of Economics the next fall. The idea of going overseas to study really intrigued me. But the professor running the program was only taking ten students, and you had to have a 4.0 to go. I had a solid 2.85

and the program was full. But I was persistent and the vision of me going was solidly planted in my mind, so I tagged along, uninvited, to the first meeting. There I asked the professor, Mr. Honkalehto, if I could be on a waiting list. He said he didn't have one, but he would put me on it anyhow. "Well, okay, but don't get your hopes up," were his precise words.

Turns out that the professor was an avid swimmer. I had never noticed him at the pool before, but now saw him at nearly every one of my practice sessions. That's how synchronicity works. . . . I'd wave or go over, and we'd chat it up at the pool.

The next meeting came. Though still uninvited, I went anyhow. That was my MO for two months. After the physics BS, I was focusing more on positive self-talk because self-doubt hadn't served me at all. Negative self-talk and doubt had turned me into a quitter. I was hell-bent on changing that story.

Then one day, near the end of the semester, I got a call from the professor. "Mark, good news. One of the students hasn't shown up to the last two meetings, and I can't get in touch with him. Are you still interested in going?"

"Heck, yeah!" I got the slot.

A week later, I bumped into the guy who no-showed, and he accused me of stealing his spot.

I looked at him and said, "I didn't steal anything. You lost it yourself. Sorry."

The Mark who dropped out of physics would not have had the confidence to pull off any of that. The same voices and emotions were still there, suggesting I wasn't good or smart enough. But I just decided to ignore them, to deny them energy and to change the story.

You, too, have the power to take control of the emotions that originate as thoughts. And you must do so for any negative ones, as your well-being depends on it. But before you can do this, you must first acknowledge them and name them. Sometimes it is a slap in the face like a quit or other fail that helps you identify the emotional patterns that are holding you back from your Uncommon Life. This work will help you avoid future self-induced slaps in the face.

It's time to master your emotional mountain!

WHAT ARE EMOTIONS?

Emotions are sensations that make us feel a certain way, think a certain way, react a certain way, and act a certain way. They come with a series of components that can be physiological (increased heart rate), expressive (flinching), mental (creating focus), behavioral (causing the urge to flee), phenomenological (sick feeling in the stomach), or evaluative (deciding something's dangerous). They can be short-lived, such as joy, or drag on like grief. They can arise out of nowhere, as panic does, or exist as a disposition, in the case of hostility. Fear of encountering a bear in the woods begins in your gut, while fear of losing the championship game is a cognitive process. Hate is a conscious emotion, while regret is unconscious. And some emotions provoke reactions, as in the case of rage, while others, such as melancholy, are resistant to action.[1]

Though emotional energy can be stored anywhere, including outside the physical body, sensations, such as surprise, originate in the body, generally the belly. They are basic human responses to a pleasure or pain stimulus. However, our reaction to any stimulus can produce thoughts that trigger a secondary emotional response because these sensations are translated through the nervous system to the brain, where some cognitive meaning is associated with them. A sibling leaping at you from around a corner wearing a goaltender mask sends the sensation of terror from your gut to your mind, which can then be experienced in the body as a shrill scream (or your sibling might experience it as a punch to the nose as my brother did).

But sensations can also illicit a cognitive reaction that can be specific to your natural state of being. An example would be taking a sip of scalding hot tea. *Shit, that's hot!* is a common reaction to the pain stimulus. But then some of us let our thoughts and emotions run wild after that with phrases like *I'm such a dumbass,* or *Crap . . . I hate my life.*

Or consider the reaction to a different type of sensation: *That idiot just cut me off! The universe is so against me today. Crap . . . I hate my life.* The jarring effect of being cut off in traffic led to thoughts that then were experienced as emotions—the exact emotion as the scalding hot tea example. Think about that.

Sensations that lead to thoughts that are then experienced as emotions happen so fast, they almost co-arise and work together. This is possible because the mind has both a cognitive and emotional capacity. Therefore, emotions are not just sent to the brain from the body (*Shit, that's hot!*), but also conceived from thought (*Crap . . . I hate my life.*), which we then experience back in the body (as self-pity, discouragement, anger, frustration, or hopelessness).

Here's another great example: You spot an old friend. As you close the gap, you recognize the person with him. *Oh, look, it's my ex!* Your initial reaction is shock, which shoots up from your gut to your mind. But then, you think about it. Your ex looks great. Plus, you've always respected this friend. Does your friend see something in your ex that you missed? Suddenly, you're jealous. *Is it hot in here?* That secondary emotion was borne from thought. Now you're mad at both these individuals, even though you dumped your ex, you're in a new relationship, and you're wildly in love. Shock originated in your gut, but the jealousy and anger was all you, coming from the subsequent thoughts you allowed yourself to experience in your body.

Whether they originate in the gut or in the mind, we experience emotions all the time. The difference is our conscious mind has control over the latter—the emotions that originate from thought. This thought-driven emotional process is what creates our natural state of being, our personality, and our experiences, which turn into our memories. Once we become aware of this body-mind connection, we can then identify the emotions we've cognized and start to manage them.

This is our area of focus.

CIRCUMSTANCE OR SABOTAGE?

Every moment of your life is driven by emotions. You may not be able to stop a sibling from leaping out of a dark corner dressed like Jason on Halloween, but you can choose how to act, or react, based on the emotions your mind has contextualized. Once you recover from the shock, you can choose to laugh or be angry or exact your revenge. But the choice is yours.

None of us would choose to live with an emotion like hostility as our natural resting state if we thought we had control over it. We do! We have control over emotional states that have monopolized our personality. Worry, sadness, fear of failure, worthlessness, anger, guilt—we experience these emotions only because we have succumbed to our monkey mind.

I wasn't consciously aware of how self-doubt had been driving my life in high school and early on in college. It certainly didn't dawn on me that I had control over it until I talked to Chris. But his comment about the physics test woke me up. In that moment, I realized that I had created the emotional climate that led to dropping the class. Turns out the only test I'd failed was the one the Universe had given me on resiliency. Had I done nothing and just kept studying, logic suggests I could've ended the year with an A in physics. But then I may have gone on to be a doctor and wouldn't have written this book. This gets complicated, doesn't it? But the story is illustrative for the purposes of this section.

Many of us blame circumstance for setbacks because we've never analyzed our go-to emotions that comprise our personality and our natural emotional default state. I blamed going to a basic public school in a small town for feeling less intelligent than my peers. I chalked up doing poorly on the physics test to not understanding the concepts—and for getting a professor who didn't give a crap about me. Most of the time we don't realize we are sabotaging ourselves.

I bet you're now thinking of all the ways you've self-sabotaged in the past. Don't waste your time. We all have done it. The point is that this is excellent news! The lightbulb just went on and you can now change that story.

When I started at Colgate, I had a weak self-concept. When the harsh reality of this story became clear to me, I took measured steps to change my internal dialogue to *I'm smart. I'm learning more every day. I'm going to succeed.* Then, when I encountered the London study opportunity, instead of thinking: *I'm only a B student,* I overrode the negative self-talk with: *This is part of my future. I'm the right person for this group. I got this.* Getting accepted to the program further reinforced my newfound sense of the power of positive self-talk.

It took me several more years, however, to climb out from the negative deficit I had dug and rewrite the false story about my true potential. But, by the time I entered my MBA program at NYU's Stern School of Business immediately upon graduating from Colgate, I was easily able to get straight As. Positive self-talk and emotionally charged imagery had not only given me courage, but it also upped my grade point average.

Most of us are on emotional autopilot, sabotaging ourselves but unaware that we have the power to take back the reins. We call ourselves stupid or stubborn or lazy or hotheads or victims of circumstance because we've never examined our body-mind connection. We accept these emotions as who we are because we didn't know we had a choice.

Now, you know. The choice is yours.

The next four exercises in the Emotional Mountain section will teach you how to master the emotions derived from thought to build emotional resiliency.

But, to master this mountain, you must first break down what's not working . . . and then rewrite your story, building it from scratch. It's a process, and I want you to cut yourself a break along the way. Be consistent and be committed and you'll get there.

EXERCISE 7
Morning Mantra

With journal in hand, find a comfortable place to sit down and meditate.

Do ten minutes of box breathing.

Now that your mind is clear, think about your top two or three go-to emotions. What are they? Do you have a dominant emotional default state? If you haven't already guessed, one of my go-to emotions was shame. My thinking mind made me a victim of all circumstances that didn't bend my way. And my state of being was dominated by a feeling of "not enough." I lacked self-worth.

Feel free to jot down your go-to emotions. Note: don't be afraid of what comes up for you, as we're fixing it!

1.

2.

3.

Now jot down your dominant emotional resting state(s). This is not necessarily a heavy emotion. Maybe you're natural resting state is happy. If so, write it down. Or, maybe you have conflicting resting states that you boomerang back and forth from, such as contentment and guilt.

1.

2.

Next, create a morning mantra, or a few. Keep 'em simple and snappy, so they're easy to remember and bring a smile to your face.

1.

2.

3.

Many people lose the day as soon as they wake up. You're no longer in that category, as we put an end to that nonsense in the Mental Mountain section. Now, you rise conscious of your thoughts. But have you noticed that you start to lose your emotional balance before you finish your first cup of coffee or as soon as you check your email?

Start doing your new mantra every morning, right after you open your eyes. Set your alarm for two minutes earlier if you need to—that's all it takes! But the key here is consistency. Commit to this daily.

Over time, the morning mantra will serve you throughout the day when you're in the trenches.

This emotional balancing process has some resemblance to metacognition meditation (which we'll get to in Part IV). But rather than just starting to count from one (again) when your mind wanders, like with the Zen counting practice, you connect and reconnect to your witnessing self with a positive, personalized mantra as you go about your day.

In the next chapter, we're going to identify where fear and courage reside in our bodies and learn how to strengthen courage and starve fear. Then, we're going to examine neural pathways in the brain, *behavioral loops*, and discover how to eradicate negative loops by intercepting them with positive self-talk and creating new pathways.

8

FEED COURAGE

I n 1975, Lee Elder became the first African American to play in the Masters Tournament. And that was just the beginning for this brave pioneer.

Born in Dallas, Texas, in 1934, the youngest of ten and orphaned by age nine, Elder was raised by his aunt till the age of sixteen. On his own after that, he started caddying, and playing golf for money on the side. Despite the Caucasian-only clause that barred Blacks from competing on the American professional circuit, Elder traveled the country, hustling and refining his game.

Two years before the racial prohibition was removed from Professional Golfers' Association (PGA) bylaws, Lee Elder turned pro. It was 1959, and he set out on the United Golfers Association (UGA) tournament trail for African American players. By 1968, in an interview, he commented, "I think a lot of guys would have given up by now." But Elder kept going.

When he broke the race barrier and played his first Masters, making golf history in 1975, famed sportswriter Jim Murray of the *Los Angeles Times* wrote: *"What Lee Elder was born with was a lot of patience, determination, guts, and willpower. You can't play golf without all four of these."*

After numerous PGA Tour championships, among many other wins and achievements, Elder received the Bob Jones Award in 2019 for distinguished sportsmanship, the highest honor given by the UGA.

Elder not only broke impossible race barriers in the sport of golf, he paved the way for all African Americans.[1]

Lee Elder had an Uncommon Life because he had mastered his emotional mountain despite an entire country telling him he wasn't allowed to even participate due to the color of his skin.

THE TALE OF TWO WOLVES

The Cherokee culture believes that two wolves reside in us all. For those of you who have read my other books or gone through my programs, yes, I'm retelling this resonant Native American parable. It's the best darn metaphor out there for our purposes and lays the foundation for all our work.

The fear wolf lives in our mind. It's nasty, dark, gloomy, cynical, envious, and in constant need of attention and feedback. It's responsible for all our jealous, judging, angry, doubting thoughts. It's always finding fault with self and others and thrives on false beliefs that lead to self-limiting concepts. The fear wolf eats *I'm not enough* for breakfast.

The courage wolf resides in our heart. It's associated with feelings of goodness, abundance, optimism, compassion, gratitude, and high self-esteem. It feeds on positive imagery and kind words of forgiveness and encouragement. When fed over time, courage wolf transforms into unconditional love of self and others, and a limitless self-concept.

The parable goes that a grandfather tells his grandson about the two wolves that live inside us, and he explains how they're at war. The boy then asks, *"Grandfather, which wolf wins?"*

"The one you feed the most," the grandfather replies.

I'm not sure if Lee Elder knew this tale, but his life story— his perseverance and optimism—epitomize what one can achieve when they feed the courage wolf and starve fear.

In this chapter, I'm going to teach you about the types of fear we manifest internally so you can understand the difference between real and irrational fear. Then, I'm going to equip you with skills to eradicate irrational fear.

REAL FEAR VS IRRATIONAL FEAR

When I was seventeen, I went hiking in the Adirondacks with my friend, Wynn. He and I decided to go off-trail and summit Whiteface Mountain by traversing up a granite scar that gave the mountain its name. We spent much of the time with two feet and at least one hand on the rocks, speeding right along, until we hit a section of vertical rock surrounded by deep brush. We looked fifty feet up . . . and fifty down, and then noticed a ridge the size of a quarter running across near us. So we decided to cross that and find a safer route up on the other side. I had not done much rock climbing, but the area we needed to cross was only about fifteen feet. I told myself: *I got this.* Wynn, a seasoned climber, scampered across the rock face with no fanfare.

Then I started inching my way across, breathing deeply and focusing. Soon I hit a spot where the handhold was just a pinch. Suddenly I felt my center of gravity shift away from the rock. The pit in my stomach preceded awareness that I had lost the hold with my right hand, and I was beginning to fall. Things immediately went into slow motion, my heart skyrocketed into my throat. And I knew death was likely imminent.

If you fall off a cliff, gravity wins. If you jump out of an airplane and the parachute doesn't open, you're in trouble. If you go underwater and your gear doesn't work, you'd better be trained. If you drive down a highway at eighty miles an hour and start to skid, that's real danger. I had friends at the Vegas concert where some nutcase sniper started shooting people. They were in life-threatening peril and experienced real fear.

Real fear triggers the stress response in your central nervous system: adrenaline surges and epinephrine releases, blood retracts to your core, your heart rate elevates, and your senses light up. These physiological effects help you take immediate action to protect yourself or others from danger.

Unfortunately, people put themselves through that very same experience with fear that's not real, not life-threatening.

Irrational fear is one of many forms of resistance that will cause you to want to quit or prevent you from pursuing your goals in the first place.

You could be facing a big decision to launch an audacious business. Because of the story you have built around this, there is a set of expectations: You may fail. You could be ruined financially. Your reputation could tank. Maybe you worry you're not smart enough, good enough, or as able to succeed as some other hotshot entrepreneur. This irrational fear slowly takes you over. You lose sleep night after night and end up with adrenal fatigue or an ulcer by the end of the ordeal.

Irrational fear is not based in reality. Yet, it triggers the same physiological reactions as if you were sailing toward the earth with a chute that won't open. Your sympathetic nervous system lights up and your fear wolf howls. Losing your reputation is not the same as receiving a death threat. Yet, both could give you an ulcer.

Throwing up before a blind date, unraveling after the term paper you wrote gets lost on your computer, speaking publicly for the first time, imagining you're going to fall during your dance concert (when you've never fallen before), freaking out about whether your newly published book will make the bestseller list, obsessing over getting old—these are irrational fears.

When I scampered across that rock face, if the fall were only two feet down and my sympathetic system shot into overdrive when I lost my grip, I would have experienced irrational fear. Or if Wynn had roped and anchored with precision, the fear would have also been irrational because I would have fallen only few feet until the anchor held me. If I worked hard to write a term paper, forgot to save it, and my computer crashed, that would suck. But I'm in no real danger. Death is not imminent if my paper is late. If I throw up before going on a blind date, it's because I let illogical fear-based thoughts travel from my mind to my stomach.

There are countless things in life that can trigger these irrational fear-based reactions. They are all roadblocks to success. And let me reiterate: the body does not distinguish between real fear and the fear your monkey mind drums up. Remember how relaxed you felt when you imagined yourself on a beautiful beach with your best buddy? Now remember how nervous you got during the "shark in the water" example? The body only knows what the mind tells it.

IRRATIONAL FEAR AND BEHAVIORAL LOOPS

Because our default mode network slants toward negativity (it's downright paranoid), since 80 percent of our thoughts are repeats, and because irrational fear is the byproduct of most of this, our brain has a maze of fear-based thought and behavioral loops.

Feeding your fear wolf always sends you on a downward performance spiral. All it takes is one nasty, negative thought that's self-limiting or derived from irrational fear when you wake up in the morning or check your email or sip your mid-morning tea before it's cooled down, and you've kicked off a fear loop.

Once the fear loop is activated, it's hard to put that genie back in the bottle. Then, as you go through your day, events trigger this belief track, such as the perceived failure on a physics test. It could be a dirty look or someone cutting in line at the grocery store. Maybe you tripped in public and now you're embarrassed. You could be facing a situation that you're inadequately prepared for or even an unknown situation.

But, if you're not free-falling backward off a cliff, you're likely suffering from irrational fear, compliments of your monkey mind. Whatever the trigger event, it wakes up a subconscious pattern with its pet negative self-talk, which is lurking in the shadows just waiting to sabotage you. This negative self-talk stokes negative imagery, which gives rise to fear-based negative emotions, and now you're trapped in a closed system that's looping around and around. This can be short-lived or resurface all day (and every darn day!). And every time you run this track, you carve the limiting belief deeper into your synaptic physiology. You're literally deepening neural pathways and neurobiological reactions in your body that become harder to escape the longer you stay in them.[2]

"*Practice makes perfect.*" This phrase applies to bad habits and negative thoughts too. It can take months or years of work to override these negative loops. Don't let fear ruin your life . . . transform fear into courage instead.

When you begin to feed the courage wolf, you enact a new transformation process that starves the fear wolf. In the beginning, these false beliefs and weak self-concepts don't just vanish, but you become aware of their existence and that they're false. This is a big win. Then, the next time you experience a trigger event, you can interdict the loop before the false belief creates weak thinking, undesirable emotions, and even weaker, fear-based actions. You instead redirect your mind to positive self-talk, and then over time you will reinforce that self-talk with empowering emotions. This de-conditions the fear-based reactionary conditioning and leads to more positive and uncommon results.

This is the three-step process to intercept negative self-talk (starve fear and feed courage):

1. Intercept the negative. After the trigger event, notice where your mind wants to go and say, "Stop."

2. Now, instead of launching into your usual negative self-talk of *I'm stupid* or *Why does this always happen to me?* say, *I'm strong, I've got this.* Or try, *This just happened, but it's not about me.* Don't own the negative. You don't have *that* much power. This can seem awkward, or you may even want to resist it because you're used to feeling stupid or carrying the blame. (Your go-to emotions are ready to jump in and take over.) Keep doing it, anyway.

3. Add positive feelings if you can. If not, "stake it till you make it." Stake your position in positive terrain. Imagery helps with this. Imagine yourself as positive and courageous in whatever situation triggered the fear loop. Once you get the hang of interdicting the fear loop by using a positive interdiction statement and mantra ("I've got this, easy day, I've got this, easy day" is one of

my go-to mantras), then you will begin to experience yourself as someone who can tackle that, and any, situation.

Recall that when you can see it in your mind, and feel it strongly as "done," then you can speak of it as a done deal, and then you just go do it. That is winning in your mind before stepping into the battle. You must believe you are a person who is competent and confident in any area you decide to focus your attention. This is how you create a transformation loop—an open system that intercepts the fear loop's closed system and inserts new language, positive imagery, emotions, and energy, altering your self-concept.

Each time you practice this it gets easier and easier, until you've carved new neural pathways and created a new reality, one where the *courage loop* is your norm and fear no longer has a hold on you.

Feeding your courage wolf makes long-term goals possible. If something matters to you at all, you've got to implement internal dialogue that generates positive "can do" feelings, regardless of your present circumstances. If you do so successfully, your courageous, positive attitude will be telegraphed to other leaders, teammates, and decision makers. They'll see you as confident, reliable, and a high performer. They'll also be more inclined to help you with the lofty goals you've set, just as Professor Honkalehto did for me for the London study group.

Feeding your courage wolf is equally powerful in boosting your performance in short-term situations, too, such as during a crisis, a sporting event, or any kind of tight deadline. Positive self-talk literally strengthens your physical body and focuses your mind. (Our bodies only know what we tell them!) It encourages your emotions to be more powerful, and stokes your desire to win. It will help you discover vast reserves of energy and resiliency you didn't know you possessed. It makes the uncommon possible.

The courage loop creates a self-reinforcing spiral of success where you experience the reality of your 20X potential, setting the stage daily for emotional resilience to last a lifetime.

Lee Elder became a professional golfer several years before the Civil Rights Act was passed in 1964. He had a vision—and history, the law, and a sea of encircling racists weren't going to stop him from achieving his dream. But there were a lot of good people who saw his drive, felt his courage, supported his efforts, and cheered him on. Focus and determination emanate from the courageous.

IRRATIONAL FEAR IS CONQUERED THROUGH ACTION

It's common for fear to provoke you to do things you shouldn't, or to convince you to avoid things you should embrace. It's uncommon to commit to overcoming them.

You can learn to be calm in the face of irrational fear by accepting it for what it is, just a signal from your nervous system. Take it one step further and think of it as a friend reminding you to step up your game and tap into the 20X potential that lives inside. Then, intercept the story or negative thought that triggered it. Redirect it to your positive mantra.

I've got this, easy day. Day by day, in every way, I'm getting better and stronger. And be kind to yourself moving forward.

But know that to overcome fear you must develop courage. You do that by challenging yourself to do the uncommon . . . do things that scare you, that you've never done, and go where you've never gone, and meet people you've never met. This will really challenge you initially but, each time you repeat these exercises, you'll be reinforcing your courage loop, while the weeds start to cover your fear loop for lack of use.

Doubt is eliminated through action alone. Sometimes, that means kinetic action (physical stuff), but other times you will need non-kinetic action: thinking, visualizing, and breathwork. Both types of action minimize your risk by maximizing your preparation. And don't forget to accumulate evidence that points to truth instead of using falsehoods and idiotic assumptions to forge your path.

Develop the expectation for success, not failure. That way, failure becomes just one of the things that happens along the way, like stopping for gas or meeting an old friend for coffee.

DON'T BE A LONE WOLF

Remember: Life is not a footrace. The journey *is* the main thing. Also, you shouldn't go it alone. In fact, even if you can make it on your own, you won't be as fulfilled, nor will you make even a fraction of the positive impact on others that you have the potential to. So don't focus only on the destination and don't strive alone.

When I was on that rock face, I was safe one moment, then falling to certain death an instant later. I lost my third point of contact and both hands had lost their grip on the ledge. A cold wind of knowingness that this was it, the last moments of my life, blasted through my body. The fear was real, not of death itself, but that I wouldn't be there for my wife and family.

Suddenly and miraculously, I felt my right hand pressing back onto the rock. *God, is that you?* I wondered. No, it was Wynn. He'd had the foresight to stage himself to help me if I had any issues, ready to act. He held on to a tree, reached over the precipice, and pushed hard against the back of my hand, allowing me to reclaim my hold. That was all that was needed to regain my balance. Two or three scoots to the right, I grabbed his hand, and he hauled me to safety. I looked at him and said quietly, "Thanks," and we continued our journey.

That was that.

Wynn's small action changed the trajectory of my life and taught me a powerful lesson about facing fear realistically. And I learned the difference between real and irrational fear instantaneously, but I also discovered that I needed a teammate. Had my teammate Wynn not been there for me I would have fallen to my death. In the SEALs, we call our training partner our *swim buddy*. The swim buddy is responsible for your life, and your success. Who's your swim buddy . . . your Wynn? We can't become uncommon alone.

At some point along your path, you'll slip or trip. In fact, you will fall a lot and need to learn to expect it; embrace the suck and learn quickly from the falls. Every time it happens, when you get back up, seek support from a swim buddy with more skill and confidence, someone who's been to the place you want to go. Learn to learn from their failures as well as successes. When you feel consumed by terror and start falling again, your teammate will press your hand back on the rock. Over time the fear will subside as your courage wolf gets fed.

EXERCISE 8
Practice Feeding Courage

Grab your journal, find a quiet place, and sit comfortably.

Use box breathing for five or ten rounds to still your mind and connect to your witness. Now, think of the most recent time you were afraid. Watch the entire event unfold in your mind. Make sure you can feel the fear that you felt when it first happened. Now go through this checklist and journal any insights:

1. Assess the source of your fear or anxiety: Is it around loss? Not having enough? A desire to control what you can't? Write it down.
2. Now take a minute to adopt the attitude of im-

permanence, as life is always changing. (*"This too shall pass."*) Remember: fear is your ego paralyzed by the thought of loss and trapped in a you-are-not-enough loop, or it's just flat-out tripping because it's not in control.

3. Eradicate fear, doubt, or anxiety by moving toward the source of that fear mentally. Create a visualization where you conquer the fear by dominating the situation.

4. Now, reflect on what you can do to interdict this fear loop for good.

   a. It might mean closing the skill gap.

   b. It might mean taking different steps to properly prepare next time.

   c. It might mean committing more consistently to your morning mantra and concentration practices.

5. Commit to taking this first step by writing it down now.

6. Develop positive self-talk for this specific skill or event. Write down your mantra or phrases so you commit them to memory. (This will come back to you when you do it "for real.")

7. Practice your new visualization daily and interdict any fear when it arises. You can do this by box breathing and redirecting your mind to your mantra.

When practiced consistently, the information in this chapter creates an energetic shield for you, an insurance policy against negative energy. Every time you feed the courage wolf, you're charging up your energetic shield against negativity. When you stop feeding your courage wolf, you drop your shield, and the arrows of negativity start penetrating your system.

Resistance often presents itself as myriad intangible and material challenges that threaten to trigger fear. But if you keep connecting and aligning with your purpose, have faith that it is the right path for you, and feed your courage wolf, resistance is futile. Your train will stay on the track, charging toward your destiny. The obstacles will begin to disappear like gossamer images in front of you. When you get to the other side—and feeding courage becomes second nature—you'll realize that those obstacles weren't all that big after all.

In the next chapter, I'm going to train you how to rewrite your origin stories to stop internal triggers before they have a chance to enter the mouth of the fear wolf.

9

REWRITE YOUR STORY

You're just beginning to script the new story of your future. Congrats! But no matter how good you are at overcoming fear to unlock your 20X potential, unless you've done the deep work, your emotional past will rise to sabotage your results. One of my mentors, Gary Kraftsow, Founder and Director of the American Viniyoga Institute, once said to me: *"If you're an asshole and you meditate for twenty years but neglect your emotional development, you're just going to be a more focused asshole."*[1]

It's true. If you haven't re-scripted the negative stories of the past that are locked in layers of emotional energy, you might get rich and you might get famous, but you'll still be an asshole, coward, bully, liar, whiner, self-saboteur, or quitter.

Exalted leaders most often fall because they ignore their emotional development. You've seen this. You revere a celebrity, athlete, or political figure only to discover they've been hiding a drug or gambling problem, or they were cheating on their partner or embezzling money, or they're being accused of sexual assault, or worse. With the rise of the internet and social media, it feels like we see instances of this weekly.

In the seventies, American scientist Candace Pert made a historic discovery that would have a profound impact on our understanding of this mind-body connection. She identified molecules that unlock brain cells to allow oxytocin, dopamine, morphine, and other neuropeptides, neurotransmitters, and opiates to enter.

Since then, scientists have discovered these "unlocking" molecules, called *neuropeptide receptors*, throughout the body. This network links the brain, endocrine system, immune system, and nervous system. Through Pert's research, we now know that *"Our emotions are a kind of nexus between our mind and our matter, carrying messages back and forth and influencing both."*[2] This means we cannot escape our emotions. They are the bridge between every system in our bodies. If we can't escape them, we'd better learn to work with them to benefit our life rather than destroy it.

Pert found scientific proof that when we think negative thoughts, chemicals are released that travel to *and permeate* other systems in our bodies, weakening both our physical health and psychological well-being. Thinking happy thoughts is healing. Happiness, satisfaction, joy, physical and intellectual pleasure: these emotions release dopamine, serotonin, oxytocin, and endorphins, often referred to as *"the quartet of chemicals responsible for happiness."*[3] When we consciously create positive thoughts, we can literally boost our mental and physical well-being in the same manner. Over time, this is how we heal and become emotionally mature.

Another way to up your emotional development is through exercise. Physical exertion makes us feel good, which in turn creates more positive thoughts.[4] Hopefully you're already doing this, so you have a head start.

We have also seen that another way to rewire the brain is through meditation. Both orbitofrontal and hippocampal regions have been implicated in emotional regulation and response control. Researchers believe larger volumes in these regions in meditating versus non-meditating brains may account for the meditator's singular ability to cultivate positive emotions, retain emotional stability, and engage in mindful behavior. And, hopefully you're doing this too!

Positive self-talk √

Proper nutrition, sleep, and exercise √

Meditation √

Morning mantra √

Feed the courage wolf √

The physical and mental training in this book is fairly easy to enact if you think about it. Once you commit to it, climbing the physical and mental mountains just requires you replace some old habits of thinking and doing with some new ones. But mastering your emotional mountain requires a special level of dedication. Fear and negative ruts almost always stem from your BOO shadow self, which is *not so obvious* to you until someone like me asks you to examine it.

So, as you embark on developing your new skills and continue to starve your fear wolf and feed courage, what will trip you up is the emotional energy from your origin stories that run all the way back to early childhood—the root cause of your shadows.

I'm going to teach you how to deconstruct your old stories and rewrite new ones, so that you can eradicate negative internal triggers, release happy chemicals at will on a regular basis, and have one less thing to worry about on your journey to mastering your emotional mountain.

We are putting an end to that BOO drama now.

BOO!

Your default mode network keeps bad memories on hand and at the ready to save you from saber-toothed tigers and a nasty neighbor. Sensations are associated with these painful memories (i.e., events, attitudes, or ways of being from your past). Your judgmental, fear-based thinking mind has attached disempowering meaning to these sensations. These disempowering emotions that prowl around your subconscious waiting to pounce comprise your BOO.

Often an internal stimulus, such as a feeling of danger, which can be real or perceived (in the case of a dark but familiar hallway), will trigger a cognitive flag of potential harm and the emotion of fear. Other times, an external stimulus, such as the sight of someone with a menacing look, will trigger the thought of potential harm, followed by the emotion of fear. A red baseball cap could trigger a frightening memory, and fear will surface as a result.

Every emotion we experience has a trigger. You smell an apple pie cooking and think of your grandma. Most of you are thinking, *Aw.* But what if your grandma was the worst? What if she was terrifyingly mean and had bad breath to boot? The smell of apple pie might make you nauseated or give you the creeps. You're stressed at work, and someone tells you to "chillax." This is the term your significant other uses when they think you're being emotional. Now you're pissed—and not just because you find the word *chillax* ridiculous.

These varying examples demonstrate that your body-mind system works as an integrated whole. You can't avoid emotions. They will always be there to either trip you up or support your efforts. You may have learned to suppress them, deny them, project them, or disconnect from them, but they are still there and an integral part of you.

Okay, so let's review this chain of events: What we know so far is that our brain's cognizing capacity re-cognizes a stimulus, and our thinking mind immediately pegs some meaning to it. Then we experience our thinking mind's "interpretation" of these sensations as emotions in our body.

The stimulus can be caused by an external trigger (menacing look) or come from internally stored BOO (the apple pie/scary grandma association). But emotions triggered by your BOO are powerful and disruptive forces that thwart forward goal or growth progress.

The good news is we have already learned how to intercept these thoughts, which are caused by internal or external stimuli, by interrupting the closed fear loop with positive self-talk, thereby turning it into a transformational courage loop. This is one way we can create new neural pathways over time and up our emotional development.

Got it? Yes, I've got it, too, but I've worked up a sweat just thinking about all these steps.

So, here's my question: Do you want to spend your life constantly telling your mind to "*STOP!*" every time it's triggered?

You do not.

Here's an alternate idea: How about we stop the stimulus at the source, so it never evolves into negative, self-defeating commentary that we must then manage?

CONTROLLING THE NARRATIVE

As discussed, our BOO is my term for hidden emotional energy and trained mental biases that can trigger reactionary behavior.

The reason this behavior may not be obvious to you is because it runs as a behavioral algorithm in the "background" of your mental-emotional operating system. People make comments about the BOO of others all the time, without even realizing they're doing it. "*She's quick to cry.*" "*He's a hothead.*" "*They always have their guard up.*" The therapy professional calls this our *shadow self*. Shadow issues are hard to get a direct look at—but they cast an enormous and ominous shadow on our lives. Often, you can see someone else's shadow clearly—the *background* of others is *more obvious to you*—but your own shadow remains hidden from your view.

BOO is neither positive nor negative in and of itself. It just is. BOO is the culmination of the conditioned thoughts, beliefs, and reactions we have adopted since early childhood—the story we live without question. But when we adopt negative beliefs and reactions because we were never equipped to deal with trauma, then that BOO has negative consequences. And, in case you think you're special or immune, stand by. . . .

That is BOO too! In my experience, everyone has it and it can't be avoided.

The point is that if we are committed to growth, then we must examine it. Eradicating negative BOO is necessary to unlock your full potential, to find complete fulfillment.

Emotional pain is often more traumatic than physical pain. Physical breakdowns and injuries can be healed with time and effective medical care. Emotional pain is permanent if you don't know how to process it. It will show up again and again. Just when things seem to be going well, there it is, bringing you down. It can be triggered by trauma, such as the death of someone you know or love. It can be triggered by stress, lack of sleep, poor nutrition, the sweet smell of a freshly baked pie. You will have to face, feel into, and resolve past wounds to master your emotional mountain, and this work takes courage.

Maybe your family withheld love from you, and that trauma was not something you knew how to handle. (What young person would?) This BOO will negatively impact important areas of your life later on. Shadow is found where the light of awareness is blocked.

So, how do you catch a glimpse of your shadow if you are not aware of it?

Look back at your life over the last month or year. What patterns do you see? If they are not obvious to you, ask someone who cares to point them out. If they love you, they will be kind while telling you the truth. Find an instance where your shadow showed up to torch things.

Was there a destructive action you regret? Was there a point where you acted like a victim? Did you do something stupid? Did you engage in crude conversation or behavior? Did you shy away from something that you knew you should do? Did you push people away? Did you stay silent when you saw something worth speaking out against? Did you say something that you wish you hadn't? Are you stuck in a negative relationship at work? At home? Have you been dressing like nothing matters (think velour sweat suit)? Any of these could indicate you have a shadow issue to work on.

BOO can be detected in your body language and your everyday dialogue with those in your peer groups. *"You're so hot. I wish I had your body."* Or *"I can't do it. Will you do it for me?"* Or *"Go away. Leave me alone."* These words reflect low self-worth and, along with any sarcastic or arrogant language, indicate negative BOO.

But, because we wear personality masks, internal dialogue is an even more likely indicator of the BOO that's holding you back from greatness.

Reflect on your thoughts. Do you think about running away from something? Do you feel unsafe? Do you obsess about financial insecurity or wish you were out of debt? That is scarcity, the emotion of not feeling worthy. Do you think you are an idiot when you do something wrong? Do you wish you were smarter, stronger, more attractive? That's shame. Are you constantly thinking about sex? Perhaps you've acquired unhealthy sexual energy from your father or mother. Or worse, perhaps you were abused. These types of negative BOO patterns are rooted deep and are painful to face and overcome. Issues around money, survival, sex, power, and physical-mental health present opportunities for deeper awareness and growth. But we must do the work!

Your BOO is most transparent when you consider your relationships with others. You can easily scan for it when you think about people close to you, one at a time, and then consider the issues of money, sex, food, survival, and power.

Start by looking at the things you dislike in someone close. Projection is a common reaction to negative emotional BOO. "If you spot it, you probably got it!" Unidentified negative BOO is either repressed or projected. You will have a strong urge to point it out in the people closest to you. Jesus said, *"Why do you look at the speck in your brother's eye, but not notice the beam in your own?"* (Matthew 7:3). Good question. It's because you're projecting your own BOO onto others instead of noticing it in yourself.

To eradicate negative BOO, you must identify it first, then turn it from subject (me) to object (it). This means to stop saying things like: *"Well, that's just who I am,"* and instead, examine it like you would a shell you picked up on the beach. The shadow is revealed when viewed as an object, not an indelible part of your personality. Any object that can be observed, can be understood. A process called *recapitulation* is a useful tool to do just that.

RECAPITULATE AND HEAL

I developed a practice called *recapitulation* to help clear up shadow issues you have identified. Recapitulation is used to clear up the issues you have identified from your shadow self. The process requires courage and patience. But once you experience its power, I hope it becomes a lifelong practice. This practice isn't likely to heal deep issues in one working session. Also, it's important to focus on one issue at a time, starting with the nastiest—all your other issues likely stem from that one, anyhow!

Recapitulation is a stacked practice that draws from therapeutic techniques such as visualization, breathwork, and cognitive behavioral therapy. You've already incorporated breathwork and visualization into your routine, so this should feel like the natural next step up the emotional mountain. To reiterate: the point of this practice is to stop your BOO from controlling your reactions to the stimuli you experience all day, every day.

This is how we rewire our brains to behave in a way that complements our emotional well-being and builds resilience.

EXERCISE 9
Recapitulation

1. Get yourself into the right state of mind with your journal in your training space. Now, write down the biggest issue you've identified throughout the last year of your life. Write about the negative impact it's had. And write about what you believe to be the root cause of the emotional-reactionary patterns that keep showing up. This BOO could be attached to an origin story from your childhood. Our biggest BOO is usually the one that's been shadowing us for the longest period. (It's okay if you don't have all the answers in your first session. Do your best.)

_____

_____

_____

_____

_____

_____

_____

_____

_____

2. Now, practice box breathing for at least ten minutes.

3. Next, set an intention to clear up the shadow and ask your witnessing self (or higher power) for guidance and support. You need to get out of your head for this to work optimally. Check your ego at the door.

4. Bring the issue into your conscious awareness. Got it? Now, it's time begin the gritty work by combining two of your brain's most powerful tools: memory and visualization.

5. In your mind's eye, travel back in time by remembering events where the BOO issue tripped you up. This is part memory and part imagination (because our memories are so much imagined). You should be able to list a slew of instances.

6. Continue to "remote view" into your past, looking for emotional storms that caused you to act out, feel victimized, or weak and nonreactive. These are the moments that plague you today as anxiety, anger, or shame. And it's these moments that can cause you to continue to have unhealthy, unsatisfactory, or abusive relationships.

7. Keep tracing back deeper into your past, until you begin to identify the underlying incident(s) that are plausible root causes. When you find a genesis point, begin to objectify the situation. Separate from it and watch yourself going through it from a second person (think of yourself as you instead of me) and then third person (think of yourself as he/she) perspective.

8. Verbalize internally (or out loud): *I am not that. That's an event that happened, but I am not that.* Let go of attachment to that energy. . . . You no longer need to suppress it as you have the awareness and skillful means to deal with it.

9. Now, forgive "you" and "he/she" and any person who may have wronged you. Apologize to yourself for holding on to the negative energy for so long.

10. Merge a vision of your current, mature self with that disempowered younger self. Approach your younger self from the perspective of your higher self and reintegrate.

(What works for me is giving that version of myself a hug and merging the images, healing the "child within.") You're releasing stuck energy, and replacing it with the energy of your wiser, more mature self. In this way, you have become whole again. You just got a "do-over."

If this practice sounds esoteric, it's because it is. Most people never deal with these deep issues. They ignore them or accept them, thinking, *It is what it is.* Most people believe that who they are and how they feel is a culmination of genetics and circumstances, without considering there's a way to change all that.

Trust me, if you practice recapitulation in earnest, I know you will find that it works.

When I dealt with my issues, I found emotional trauma experienced as a child as the genesis. I had suppressed it, then became numb to it as a teenager. I came to think of that suppressed energetic state as "normal," and denied any problems. But I was not happy. I was drinking too much and couldn't maintain a relationship worth beans. I also had an absurdly high emotional pain tolerance, since I'd numbed pretty much every emotion, including joy. When your emotional pain tolerance is high, you become a doormat. And you don't even recognize it. You think everyone goes through it, and oftentimes, you think you're helping by being so open to the emotional abuse. You think you're being a good friend, an open-minded partner, and you convince yourself that the grass is never greener on the other side. These are the lies we tell ourselves to hold on to our origin stories and go-to emotions.

BOO that is identified and resolved is no longer BOO. It becomes part of your conscious awareness. When this happens, your emotional intelligence increases. You develop emotional power. Your heart, your courage wolf, oversees your actions and reactions. You make decisions based on all the evidence. You have high self-esteem and self-worth. You are happier and more content, which releases endorphins and dopamine into your system on a regular basis. And you are farther along on the path to your Uncommon Life.

In the fourth and final chapter in the Emotional Mountain section, we are going to heal our emotional wounds by understanding how regret (holding on to the past) and worry (having anxiety about the future) are preventing us from mastering our third mountain. And we're going to say goodbye to these emotions forever.

10

NO REGRETS

H ave you ever come across a Rubik's Cube and *not* had the urge to pick it up and solve at least one side? Me neither! This is because the ego mind is a problem solver. It's always thinking, 24-7. In fact, it's hooked on problem-solving to the point that it literally seeks out problems in our everyday lives just so it can feel important.

Back in 1974, in a college class in Hungary, Ernő Rubik had no idea the impact the 3D model he'd created to demonstrate movement to his students would have on the world. For starters, with forty-three quintillion variations on this six-sided design with fifty-four individual squares, it took him a whole month to solve his own puzzle, which he'd referred to as his Magic Cube. After that, when it got packaged as a toy, Rubik assumed it would only appeal to math and science geeks.[1] Boy, did he underestimate . . . everybody.

A Rubik's Cube sitting atop a lonely desktop is to our ego

mind what a big, juicy steak left unattended is to a hungry pooch. And there are over five hundred million Rubik's Cubes in circulation to back up that analogy, making it the most popular puzzle in the history of the world. The Rubik's Cube has been giving our brains something to do for five decades. And the creation of the internet and YouTube tutorials have expanded the craze exponentially.

But that ego mind of yours goes further than simply seeking out problems; it also creates them. Lots of them.

In this chapter, I'm going to teach you how to spot this pesky habit of creating problems where none exist. And then, we're going to use the skills we've already acquired to put an end to it for good.

Let's go!

TRUE REALITY IS NOT BIASED

Have you ever caught yourself doing that—creating a problem where there was none? Unless you've never been in a relationship with another human being, you've done this. It's what the mind does. It can turn anything into an issue if it pays it enough attention. *Anything.* But the mind does not need to have another person or a puzzle in front of it to create a problem. It can generate one out of thin air. Check out this: The Contentment Dilemma:

Gosh, I feel good these days. I enjoy work. My homelife is peaceful. Life has been so doable lately. I really feel the flow.

Wait a minute. . . .

Suddenly, you start thinking about this feeling of content-ment and, the next thing you know, your happiness becomes a problem that needs to be solved. *Why am I so damned happy?* It starts with "why." Then those thoughts multiply, using the whys and the hows to gather information. *How did I get so happy? How long is this happiness going to last? Will I still be happy tomorrow? Next week? On my birthday? How can I hold on to this feeling? What future obstacles could interrupt this happiness? I need to identify those and avoid them or eliminate them or . . .*

When we let our monkey mind run the show, it'll turn anything, including contentment, into a dilemma. We liter-ally think away our "inner peace" and replace it with panic, worry, and fear. We've all caught ourselves experiencing a feeling of bliss for a stint. And then, as soon as we start thinking about it, we wonder how long it's going to last. And then, we start freaking out about it going away and we find ourselves on guard, waiting for something "bad" to happen. On more than one occasion, I bet you've worried away your sunny days. We all have. Don't stress about it. Besides, you can't change that now, as it's in the past.

Though our ego mind wants us to believe this, everything is not a problem to be solved. Viewing life this way distorts the true reality of things.

True reality exists without bias and judgment. It just is. Re-ality exists without labels and emotions, even though the con-stant chatter in our mind wants to judge, attach an emotion, wants to "fix the problem." And do you want to know what's worse? Once our conscious mind has decided there's a problem that needs to be solved—and we hop on board that train—our happiness is gone. It's over because now we're thinking about it, which means we are no longer living in the moment and enjoying the bliss of things as they are. Our monkey mind has created an issue and escorted us right into a place called *If only* to solve the problem. And that place is always in a past or future mental experience.

If only I were thinner, had more money, a nicer car, the latest gadget, lived in a warmer climate, painted my house a darker shade of gray, had a better relationship with my mother, my boss, my employees. . . . If only I could fix this one thing, then I'd be happy.

Then you fix "this one thing." You buy your dream car and life is good for a stint. You're content again. Until that voice jumps back in and says something to the effect: *Hey, do you see that new problem over there?* And you make the mistake of engaging. *I do! I do see that new problem over there! . . . If only my ears were more attractive, life would be perfect.* (Oh, yes, no "problem" is off limits to your monkey mind.) And just like that, your happiness is unraveled. It found another Rubik's Cube—your big dumb ears—and it needs to start twisting. The ego mind looks for problems like a missile homing in on a target.

We unravel perfectly good relationships, create career setbacks, blow the championship game, and drop physics just by listening to this "voice in our head." We've already discussed and addressed some of this by learning to feed courage and starve fear through the practice of recapitulation. But did you know our experiences are not just affected by this higher-level self-sabotage? Get ready for this. . . .

Our monkey mind distorts our memories too! This brain of ours that's always thinking wants to not only question the perfectly fine present so that we stress about the future, it wants to change the past as well. *If only I had stopped after two drinks, not listened to my mother, finished college, started saving sooner . . . If only I had stopped eating like crap in my twenties . . .* And when we allow it to do this, our memories live on to haunt us in the form of the emotional *regret*.

FREE YOUR TRAPPED ENERGY

You may have dealt with a lot worse than I did as a child, or maybe not. In any case, my origin stories, of which my memories are a part, had me wallowing in regret for far too long.

Growing up, my dad had alcohol and anger issues, to say the least. When my brother and I would do rowdy kid stuff past bedtime, he would stomp upstairs and smack the hell out of us with a belt. My brother's bed was closest to the door, and often the steam would be blown off on him and "same to you" was my punishment. That was worse than the belt. The earliest memory I have of my childhood is of my second birthday. I was sitting in a high chair, my family was singing "Happy Birthday," and, as the cake with candles was placed in front of me, I flung it to the floor. Apparently, I was pissed at life already. At two.

As you know, childhood memories can be triggered late in life.

A few years ago, I was at a SEALFIT event on a Montana ranch. The owner asked me and a SEAL buddy to clear some rodents from the land. The small varmints were breeding out of control, creating a hazard to the land, the farm staff, and the equipment. We grabbed the .22-caliber rifles from the gun case and hopped on the ATV. It was like playing "whack a mole" at first. But then, I had killed so many of the little guys that I started to get sick to my stomach. And it was at that point that the memory of another ugly childhood incident came back to me.

I was about five years old, and I had a pet hamster. Through the barrel lens of my memories, I saw myself take the tiny animal out of the cage and throw it on the floor repeatedly. I was very angry at the time. But rather than expressing it in a healthy way, I took it out on my pet. Sad day. This memory, that many might ignore or laugh off, tore at me later in life. It made me sad, and I felt shame that I would do that to another living being.

At that point, I put the gun down and vowed to never deliberately kill another animal again.

That evening, I used the recapitulation process and re-experienced the childhood event, including the anger, shame, and guilt. What led me to kill my pet hamster, I asked? I could now see I was acting out suppressed rage at the emotional trauma I was experiencing in the home. I was a young child, and this was how I was being taught to cope.

That recapitulation led to healing and the eradication of the regret. I felt lighter.

That was my life, and those were the cards I was dealt. Forgive and move on.

Now, as an adult, I could clear up that trapped energy. Feeling my emotions and expressing them wasn't something I was able to do at five. So that suppressed energy was holding me back in ways I couldn't see but could sense and feel in the form of shame. The recapitulation practice objectified the incident, and I was able to forgive myself, *and my parents,* and move on.

For too many of us, emotional BOO that leads to anger, shame, and guilt stays buried deep inside the folds of our enigmatic mind. And the longer we go without addressing our shadows, the harder it becomes to dredge them up and clear them out. Bitterness, unhappiness, or hopelessness becomes the emotional resting state in a person whose mind is bogged down by unfortunate memories. These states are hard to break, as they are so familiar, and there's comfort in familiarity. This goes back to the definition of inertia. These origin stories have been parked in our mind for a very long time. Pushing them out takes a lot of force. But once they sail away . . .

You must let those things go to let love flow. And now you have some tools to make these changes.

NO REGRETS

Regrets are known shadow issues you haven't had the courage to resolve. They've been identified but you have neither objectified nor resolved them. You're still merged with the negative energy from the situation. Anything you ponder from the past with "*woulda coulda shoulda*" dialogue attached is a regret that's holding you back from mastery of self, or it's an unresolved issue that will lead to more regret in the future. What you focus on grows, so if you ruminate about a regret it becomes a bigger regret. Screwups, setbacks, or challenges that you didn't handle well—these happen to everybody!—this is what I'm talking about. Regrets kill your motivation moving forward and rattle your peace of mind.

Drinking to excess was a common pattern in my family, and it was common practice in the navy. I was neither exempt from this habit nor had I thought to examine the emotional BOO behind my bingeing. I was an officer and a gentleman, but one with disaster on my horizon. I had to set a higher standard. This, I should have recognized. But bingeing was a way of denying my feelings. And though I was hardly aware of it, this was how I coped. Sure enough, one night I got toasted with my small team after an op, and my commanding officer was not impressed. He ran me up the flagpole, relieving me of my leadership position for a couple of months.

For a long time, I held regret about this incident. I went from the top-ranked lieutenant at SEAL Team 3 to being fired from my platoon. The language of that regret was: *Boy, did I screw up. I should have been more disciplined. I could have controlled myself better . . . and blah, blah, blah.* That was the fear wolf story looping in my head (and it didn't help, in case you were wondering).

Back then, I identified it as a single poor choice. I couldn't see that it was a pattern arising from a shadow issue trying to smack me down again and again. When I finally found the courage to recapitulate this, I saw other alcohol-related incidents starting in my late teens. The recapitulation allowed me to see it for what it was. I identified the incident that caused the regret. I visualized the source by digging into how my shadow BOO was involved. I objectified the incident, turning "I am" into "It was." Then, I examined it objectively (like that shell on the beach). Once I understood it, I was able to eradicate it and let it go. I reframed my story. I learned a big lesson from it, after all. Then, I forgave myself, forgave others who were involved or apologized to victims of this event, and I became free to move on.

I'm going to take a minute of your time to put this practice in "list" form, because it's going to be your next exercise. This is how I released myself from the regret of getting fired at Team 3:

1. I admit to being saddened by the behavior that led to the firing.
2. I acknowledge binge drinking led to this unfortunate incident.
3. I saw that I had had a habit of bingeing on beer since my teens as a way of not facing feelings of inadequacy.
4. My parents fought a lot, and my father was angry and abusive. I've been angry about this and have felt helpless for as long as I can remember, since I was three. By my late teens, I discovered alcohol and used it to cope.

5. Getting fired from my leadership position was just one of several events that happened involving alcohol. I tell myself: *That happened because I used beer to fill a gap in my life. It wasn't my fault. I was surviving the only way I knew how. But now, I don't need it anymore.*

6. I see the incident with unbiased eyes: *This incident was valuable because it allowed me to learn about myself and become stronger.* This is the courage wolf story.

7. Finally, I forgive myself for coping with my issues in an ineffective way. I forgive myself for the negative self-image that led to using beer to manage my emotions. And I forgive my parents for not knowing a better way to manage their BOO. They are not evil people, and they did the best they could with the skills they had available.

We must objectify the BOO to end the pattern. I saw how I used alcohol to substitute for my lack of emotional awareness, and to mask pain. There are healthier approaches to addressing emotional issues, which I discovered, and which I am passing on to you. This is not a one-and-done exercise, by the way. Some issues you have to stay on like white on rice until they dissolve into the clear light of acceptance.

To free yourself, identify the memories, and then consider the root emotional trauma they point to. Then, define the trauma as an object that is not you, but outside of you. Tell this object: *You are not me, and you don't mess with my life anymore.* The energy associated with the trauma will begin to dissipate, along with regret. And the patterns that typically arise because of the suppressed energy, such as negative self-talk and bad behavior, will vanish too.

Soon enough, those habits will be eating your dust as you trek forward on the path to your Uncommon Life.

EXERCISE 10
End the Regret

What regrets are holding you back? Let's commit to ending them now.

We will start with a small one to build the skill set.

Sit comfortably with your journal. Take ten or more minutes to box breathe.

Now, follow this process in detail to end regret:

1. Identify an incident that you are holding on to in the form of regret.
2. Journal the words or actions that caused the regret.
3. Visualize their source.
4. Recapitulate by writing down how your shadow BOO (origin stories) was involved.
5. Define and visualize the incident and its emotional energy (and the BOO) as an object outside of your "I am" identity. It was not you. It was an event, a thing that happened.

6. Examine the object (of regret), denounce it, and reject it. Commit to eradicating it from your life and end the regret. Write down how you've grown because of this event.

7. Forgive yourself and any person(s) who you think harmed you. If you've harmed someone, an apology is appropriate. It's best to apologize in person, but that's neither possible nor reasonable in many situations. In some cases, years have passed. Often, it will just stir up more bad energy. You can apologize by writing a letter and then burning it, or by just voicing the apology internally too.

Bottom line: You and I don't need to be victims to our BOO or each other's BOO, whether in the form of weak stories or stored emotional energy leading to reactionary behavior. Anything we think, feel, and do is our sole responsibility.

Choose to let go of that regret to change the feelings, thoughts, and behavior associated with it. That's the uncommon mindset you need to develop to reach your full potential.

Take responsibility. Feel the pain. Then forgive and get over it. And I encourage you to acknowledge the flaws and failures of your parents, just as you acknowledge your own flaws and failures. Your family has beaucoup BOO because all humans are imperfect. If we were all perfect, the world would be boring and there would be no growth. Learn to forgive your family . . . be thankful for the positive things they did to bring you to this point in your life.

Eliminating regrets of the past will allow you to accelerate toward your destiny. Eliminating regret will increase awareness of the present moment and decrease worry about the future.

BONUS EXERCISE 2
What's Your EQ?

In 1990, psychologists Peter Salovey and John D. Mayer coined the term *emotional intelligence,* describing it as *"a form of social intelligence that involves the ability to monitor one's own and others' feelings and emotions, to discriminate among them, and to use this information to guide one's thinking and action."*

A few years later, psychologist Daniel Goleman, PhD, wrote the book *Emotional Intelligence,* where he further capitalized on the importance of emotional development and coined the term "EQ" or *emotional quotient.* Goleman argued that it wasn't cognitive intelligence, "IQ," but emotional intelligence that drove success in business. He described emotionally intelligent people as those with four characteristics:

1. *Adept at understanding their own emotions (self-awareness)*
2. *Adept at managing their emotions (self-management)*
3. *Empathetic to the emotional drives of other people (social awareness)*
4. *Adept at handling other people's emotions (social skills)*[2]

EQ gives us a new language for describing emotions as an important type of intelligence alongside IQ. I would go even further and suggest that each of the five mountains has a quotient: physical (PQ), mental (IQ), emotional (EQ), intuitive (AQ for awareness quotient), and spiritual (SQ). Assessing and developing these intelligences is the work we do in my Unbeatable Mind program, and an area of deep interest to me.

If this is intriguing to you, too, check out *Emotional Intelligence 2.0* by Travis Bradberry and Jean Greaves, and take their EQ test found within the book. Then, after a year of work, take it again. You'll be able to observe real progress as you climb your emotional mountain. This work is invaluable for developing self-awareness.

Congratulations, you've made it through the Emotional Mountain section.

MASTERING YOUR EMOTIONAL MOUNTAIN . . . *IN REVIEW*

- You understand the true nature of emotions and how they connect every system in the body.
- You've learned that every experience you have is triggered by a sensation that goes to your brain, which applies meaning to it and sends it back to your body in the form of an emotion.
- You've developed a morning mantra that you're using consistently. This mantra carries you through your day. It's at the ready to tackle all your obstacles.
- You've learned that feeding courage and starving fear will start the process of undoing the fear-based behavioral loops in your neural pathways and start the transformational process of rebuilding them as courage loops.
- You've discovered the powerful practice of recapitulation. You can now identify the root cause of your own BOO and use this practice to change your emotional resting state by traveling back in time and observing incidents where your go-to emotions from

your thinking mind have tripped you up. This will up your emotional intelligence, your self-awareness, and your self-esteem. (In essence, we dug deeper and deeper into your triggers and behavioral patterns with each chapter.)

- And you've come to understand that your brain loves problem-solving to the point that it will create problems so it has something to solve. The way to control your mind is by letting go of regret (the past) and worry (the future) so you can exist contently in present-moment awareness and stay focused on the journey to your Uncommon Life.

The next skill we are going to tackle is learning to act intuitively, spontaneously, and authentically by listening to your gut and heart brains. Leadership capacity is directly proportional to your authenticity and ability to respond to unpredictable events. Are you ready to master your Intuitional Mountain?

Let's get started!

Part IV

MASTERING YOUR INTUITIONAL MOUNTAIN

- We're going to remove the mask from the term *intuition* to gain an understanding of what it is and how it works.

- We'll study the brain-gut connection, the two types of intuition, and discover that to achieve holistic intuition we need to practice honing our outer and inner awareness.

- We'll study heart intuition and its role in our lives and relationships. And we'll take a deeper look at how to become masters of our intuition through mindfulness meditation.

11

THE POWER OF INTUITION

I n the mid-sixties, Yale undergrad student Fred W. Smith, having procrastinated long enough on his economics paper, slapped together an idea about a fleet of planes for parcel delivery across the United States. They'd fly by night and transport packages exclusively, as opposed to the then-current system, which added parcels to passenger flights. If you're not familiar with Federal Express's rise to greatness, google it. You'll find a slew of contradictions over the grade Smith got on this term paper. We don't care about his grades. What's relevant here is that, while his professor wasn't wowed by the concept, Smith had a strong sense he was onto something.

When he graduated, however, he didn't pursue this gut feeling, but went into the Marine Corps and did two tours in Vietnam. The notion of launching this company still haunted his mind and he couldn't shake it. Smith had received a several-million-dollar inheritance from his father and didn't need to risk it all on a crazy business fantasy. But he put it all into his idea, acquired substantial venture capital, just under nine figures, and set out to make his vision a reality.[1]

By 1973, FedEx was up and running. But the explosion of the auto industry created a demand for gas that forced the US to lean hard on the Middle East for oil, giving them the kind of leverage that economists had forecasted and feared. Gas went up by almost 40 percent.[2] Suddenly, the young company was losing money fast. Down to his last few thousand dollars with no investors in sight, Smith, while traveling out West, detoured to Las Vegas on a hunch, beelining to the blackjack table. He more than quadrupled his money, giving him the motivation and confidence to keep going. He acquired more funding after that.

FedEx has been hit by some hefty obstacles over the decades, all while competing against a massive government agency. But the company has always gotten back on its feet. In 2019, it raked in close to seventy billion, according to *Forbes*.[3] *"No business school graduate would recommend gambling as a financial strategy, but sometimes it pays to be a little crazy early in your career,"* Smith once wrote.

I don't think Fred Smith was crazy. I know from my own experience that it pays big-time to listen to your intuition. Smith wasn't acting irrationally when he dumped his inheritance into a business idea. He was listening to his gut . . . and it told him to take the risk. That same voice steered him into the Gambling Capital of the World when FedEx was on the verge of collapse. And gamble he did. This young entrepreneur had a natural intuitive sense that he listened to . . . and he was not going to get in the way of that intuition, or his dream.

You can do this too.

Intuition is a special kind of intelligence that is often misunderstood. As a result, some people don't believe it exists and others pay little attention to it. The term is common enough that most of us toss it around regularly, saying things like "my intuition tells me . . ." But we second-guess it and instead rely on our rational mind when making tough decisions. We may even refer to it in jest, further shutting down this important skill. When someone, like Fred Smith, is seen to be exceptionally intuitive, they are viewed as a unique being, a genius, and not like you. Some people equate a high intuitive quotient with psychic ability. An educated guess would be that psychics are very intuitive, but you don't have to be a psychic, medium, or palm reader to tune in to this skill. Psychics, like criminologists, psychologists, guidance counselors, Buddhist monks, martial artists, and people who practice mindfulness and concentration meditation, work on being present and, therefore, pay close attention to nonverbal cues, such as body language, and study their surroundings as habit. Inwardly, they pay attention to the voice in their heart-mind-gut. And they acquire this skill like any other, through many hours of practice.

In this section, we will learn about the important role intuition plays in experiencing present-moment awareness in everyday life, in goal setting, and in living your purpose with passion.

You can spend hundreds of thousands of dollars on prestigious degrees and train your rational mind to the extreme. But that won't make you more intuitive. To become more intuitive, you do it the *Uncommon* way, from the comfort of your home and at no cost other than well-invested time. Get ready to tap into your intuitional intelligence at will, as Fred did.

Time to learn to surrender to your silent inner wisdom.

TRUST YOUR GUT

When I was a junior officer with SEAL Team 3 back in the nineties, I worked with the same platoon for four years. We had missions that took us underwater or deep into the woods and jungles for weeks at a time. Most of the time we worked in silence, and because of my Zen training, I'm very comfortable just clearing my head and listening. My gut instinct about what the team was thinking or the direction we should go was exercised daily by that. I paid close attention to every sound, every movement of the team, and everything experienced internally. Over time, I found that I could sense danger or that something was wrong early. But my intuitional awareness was shared by many others in the special ops community.

In the mid-2000s, Navy SEAL MJ, a long-time meditator and martial arts instructor, was contracted by the military to lead a convoy through the heart of the Iraq War.

It was this guy's job to pay attention to any deep sensations he'd receive about roadside blasts planted along their routes, and then detour the convoy accordingly. Because he trusted that these messages were real information, and the military had literally hired him for this purpose, it was a no-brainer for the teams to trust him too. (Also, they didn't want to get their asses blown up.) When the military checked MJ's accuracy, eight times out of ten, he had been right—they'd either found and defused the roadside bomb or received news it had exploded. His intuitional ability to forecast the location of bombs on foreign territory was 80 percent accurate!

Practicing meditation and martial arts and acquiring the skills to become a SEAL all played into both my own and MJ's ability to trust our guts. We mastered skills that synced the body-mind connection, making us more attuned to nonverbal information than someone who had not refined this skill. The part of the mind that "translated" messages about the location of the bombs is often referred to as the *axis of intuition*. In scientific terms, this message center is called the *ventromedial prefrontal cortex*, where decision-making occurs. This axis of intuition is much more active and in tune with the heart-mind-gut brain centers when it is trained for some time. But there's another reason too.

Scientists and psychologists refer to the messages received from outside the body as *transrational information*. Transrational information doesn't align with the natural rules of the known physical universe. If it's cloudy out and you turn to your coworker and say, "It looks like rain," and then it rains, this statement falls within the natural laws of science. You are not (necessarily) an intuitive genius for putting two and two together and getting rain. If, on the other hand, you tell your coworker to postpone her trip back East for a day because of a constriction you felt in your gut when she brought it up, this does not follow the laws of naturally occurring phenomena. If she postpones it, and the flight she was supposed to be on crashes, you may be a master of intuitional awareness. And the message you received about the flight is transrational information—a message about the future that came from some all-knowing place. But where?

Though researchers in a variety of fields agree this exists, as you can imagine, transrational information is much less understood than hunches that are deduced by observing our environment and pulling from our unconscious memory banks to draw a natural conclusion. These types of sensations, which lead to declarations, are often dismissed by the rational mind as outrageous, unfathomable woo-woo, because there is no cause (clouds) followed by a logical effect (rain) to explain them. MJ's skills were more accepted amongst special operators, so they paid attention and saved lives.

Another term for this type of intuition is sixth sense, and a more familiar one is *women's intuition*.

How many times have we guys heard that phrase from our partner, sister, mother, or female friend? Even after I find out my wife, Sandy, was on the money with a feeling about this or that, I shake my head and think: *She didn't train in the SEALs. She hasn't sat on the Zen bench for decades. How does she know this stuff?* Though we can't exactly measure one's intuitional "levels" like we can blood volume or body mass, a study done by Dr. Daniel Amen, one of America's leading brain health experts, and nine-time *New York Times* bestselling author, says there is something to it.

Women have enhanced activity in their prefrontal cortex and hippocampus, and more blood flow in their limbic regions (emotional centers) compared to men. They are better equipped to read emotions based on facial expressions and body language for this reason. It makes sense, after all, as they have been blessed with the ability and responsibility of bringing life into the world. All these traits play into making a person appear (or even be) more intuitive. The good news, especially for the other half of us boasting the XY chromosome, is that with practice we can up our intuitional awareness to masterful levels like Smith, MJ, and your wife or girlfriend who seems to be right without having any reason to know what she is right about!

Are you familiar with the term *intuitive empath*?

You can probably guess that it's an empath with a strong intuitive sense. But why are empaths so in tune with others?

Empaths, comprising about 1 percent of the population, are emotional sponges, experiencing and reading other people's emotions without choice. Empathy comes with its own challenges, as it's exhausting managing everyone's emotions all the time. But it has its perks too. The bulk of empathic people are intuitive empaths. They detect what others are feeling *and why,* identifying the root causes of an emotional state. And they can advise how best to move forward.

Dr. Judith Orloff, a psychologist and *New York Times* bestselling author of *The Empath's Survival Guide,* tells us that empaths intuit feelings over intellectualizing them. This is how they approach and experience the world. Because they view life with their heart-mind-gut, they naturally feel more internal signals, are more giving, and are good listeners. If you know someone who seems to be everybody's go-to for counsel, who dishes out wisdom like millennials serve up slang, they are likely an intuitive empath.

Frontiers in Integrative Neuroscience studied the brain activity of a group of males and females, ages eighteen to thirty-five. Until recently, people would fill out the Questionnaire of Cognitive and Affective Empathy to determine empathic tendencies.[4] In this study, with the use of a functional MRI (fMRI), brain activity was monitored in addition to the questionnaire being filled out. By studying the results of the MRIs, researchers were able to pinpoint which people were empaths. Simple as that. The midcingulate cortex in the brains of empathic people had heightened activity with denser gray matter than the brains of non-empaths.

If you recall from Mastering Your Mental Mountain, this area of the brain is responsible for processing social information and guiding decision-making. Right-brained, left-handed creative types also have heightened activity in the same area compared to right-handed, left-brained analytical folks. Imagine how naturally in tune you'd be if you were a left-handed, female intuitive empath who practiced mindfulness and meditation? Cool.

For the other 99.95 percent of us, though, we must work at it. We're going to create uncommon intuitional awareness so you can sail toward your purpose with passion in your heart and be the kind of person from whom wisdom flows.[5]

But first . . .

WHAT DOES AN INSTINCT FEEL LIKE?

Now that you understand that heightened levels of intuition affect brain activity in the prefrontal-cortex region and can be seen on an fMRI, it's important to understand that intuition does not necessarily speak to us using words, as our critical thinking faculty does. Rather, the language of intuition can come in the form of images, sensations, gut feelings, sounds, and even smells.

So, which signals and sensations are the voice, the nudge, or the "hit" telling us how to proceed, and which sensations are just random tickles, stiff joints, gas cramps, or our monkey mind chattering away? Here is Orloff's list of what some of these physical sensations might feel like from *Second Sight*.

POSITIVE INTUITIVE HITS:

- *A sense of warmth*
- *Ability to breathe more easily*
- *Sharp clarity of hearing or vision*
- *A wave of goose bumps, tingles, or "fluttery" sensations*
- *Relaxation in the gut and shoulders*

NEGATIVE INTUITIVE HITS:

- *Icy cold hands and feet; an overall chill*
- *Twinging or clenching pain in gut or chest*
- *Nausea or acid stomach*

- *A sense of being on "high alert"*
- *Fatigue or loss of energy*
- *Onset of headache*[6]

If these sensations ring familiar, it's because intuitional intelligence exists within us all.

It's your right to tap into it. (It is, after all, tapping into you.) Orloff goes on to write: *"The benefits of listening to your instincts go far beyond making good life-or-death decisions. Living more intuitively demands that you're in the moment, and that makes for a more passionate life."*[7]

On the flip side, as with any other human capacity, if it is not used and developed, it atrophies. So, because most of us don't pay enough attention to our gut instincts to consider how they could serve us, we are not only *not practicing* on improving our natural intuitive skills, but we have lost what ability we had back when we were young, when we lived in the moment and relied readily on feelings to strategize through life.

Anytime you have a sensation that the phone is about to ring, then it does, or when you are thinking of someone and suddenly that person calls, that's transrational intuition speaking in sounds and images. Another example is the hair standing up on the back of your neck, making you switch routes on the way to work, only to find out later that there was an accident. You decide to hire the greener candidate over the more qualified applicant solely based on gut instinct. And your new hire transforms the company.

One reason SEALs are so effective is because the train-
ers do not pass off intuitive intelligence as voodoo. They acknowledge it and seek opportunities to train and refine this
special skill. SEALs rely on a combination of training, planning, intelligence, intuition, improvisation, imagination, and
luck. Most of those traits are not what you'd think of as a
Special Operations Forces' (SOF) "hard" skill. They are the
"soft" internal skills of a master warrior. Special Operators,
alone or with a small team, log dozens of hours training in
silence with senses on full alert—because this is one way to
naturally develop intuitive skills.

During one training evolution with the SEALs, I was
walking to the shooting range at our tactical training
grounds when I felt the word *stop!* in my gut strongly. It was
like a punch combined with a firm hand on my shoulder
that held me back. I Immediately froze in my tracks. A mil-
lisecond later, a gun was accidentally discharged, and the
bullet whizzed right by my ear. I felt the wind from it. Had I
not stopped, I would have been shot in the back of the head.
Gut instinct is a huge source of inspiration and wisdom that
most of us don't tap into. Why? Because you think it would
be irresponsible, or outright strange, to take orders from
sensations over our rational mind.

This is where you are wrong. And I would be dead had I
not trusted it.

Whether you've trusted this innate ability all along or have
practiced perfecting this skill like a SEAL, whether you're a
woman, an empath, left-handed, all three, or whether you're

starting at square one, you can up your game and become a master of your intuitional intelligence. I know for a fact that following your internal guidance system will radically change your life for the better. We've got this, *easy day.*

EXERCISE 11
Tune In to Your Body

We're going to do a simple sensory awareness exercise. Have your journal handy.

Let's begin with five or more minutes of box breathing.

When you're ready, begin:

- Lie down.
- Shut yourself off from your other senses. Put all your concentration and attention on your hearing. At first, the obvious things from your surroundings will capture your attention. If you're inside, maybe you'll hear a fan, or the heater kick on. The refrigerator can be a noisy contraption if you listen for it. Outside, there's the wind, birds, traffic, etc. But, as you continue to listen, you'll begin to hear what's happening inside you.
- Next, go through your entire body part by part,

just as we do when we flex and release with the traditional body scan practice, which is about focusing the mind by giving it a task (contracting and relaxing). In this exercise, we are getting in tune with the body by becoming aware of it.

- Think about your foot and just listen. Then, move up to your shin and listen, then your knee, and so on. (Don't forget to do both sides.) Move to your thighs, buttocks, lower back and stomach, transversal abdominals, chest and rib cage, hands, wrists, forearms, upper arms, shoulders, neck, head. Take your time. You can listen to your mouth, nose, eyes, and ears too. This exercise should take at least five minutes.

- Once you finish getting in tune with your body, take a few relaxed breaths and let the exercise go.

- Sit up when you're ready and write down any thoughts in your journal about the experience. Note as much detail as possible. This is how we get better acquainted with our bodies.

The more you do exercises like this, the more you'll hear and notice. Over time, you'll start to naturally pick up small signals from your body and other "remote places" throughout your day.

This develops inner awareness.

Now that we have a basic understanding of intuition, how a gut instinct feels, and how the brain responds to intuitive messages it receives from the body, in the next chapter, we will take a closer look at inner and outer awareness: how the central nervous system and enteric nervous system work together to create whole body-mind harmony and how becoming more intuitive is truth serum for your heart.

12

THE SECOND BRAIN

"If you've ever 'gone with your gut' to make a decision or felt 'butterflies in your stomach' when nervous, you're likely getting signals from an unexpected source: your second brain . . . this 'brain in your gut' is revolutionizing medicine's understanding of the links between digestion, mood, health, and even the way you think."

—JOHNS HOPKINS MEDICINE,
"THE BRAIN-GUT CONNECTION"[1]

The gut is considered the second brain because it has its own nervous system: the enteric nervous system (ENS). The ENS enables the gut to work both with the brain in the head via the spinal cord and central nervous system, and also independent of it by transmitting information via the vagus nerve. But, interestingly, about 90 percent of vagal fibers that travel between the gut and brain are *afferent*—this means the information is traveling from the ENS to the central nervous system (CNS).

Physiologically, the enteric nervous system provides local control of the gastrointestinal (GI) tract functions: secretion, barrier function, movement of fluid, regulation of local blood flow, intestinal motility, etc.[2] *(Stick with me—this won't hurt for long!)* The gut also transmits signals of nausea, bloating, or satiety to the brain.

In simple terms: these two brains talk to each other nonstop via the vagus nerve and ENS. But, as noted, most of the information is coming from the gut brain to the head brain.[3]

The head brain is obviously the CEO of the brain trust as it creates cognition with all the input from the senses as well as the gut and heart brains. The head brain integrates all that information, allowing for conscious thinking, planning, and creating, as well as the subconscious ruminations of the default mode network. This brain also manages a large number of unconscious bodily functions so you don't have to think about beating your heart, breathing in and out, or circulating your blood. The gut brain handles the unconscious management of all the functions of digestion and elimination. While doing all that, the gut brain communicates with the head brain through sensations and messages via the "vagus nerve highway." For simplicity, I will call the "head brain" the *brain* and the "gut brain" the *gut* from now on.

The brain receives enormous dumps of information from the gut and sense organs all the time. The brain needs teamwork and delegation skills to handle the workload. On its own it can't handle split-second, life-and-death decisions like pausing to let a bullet go by. And swerving out of the way of an oncoming car is certainly done without thinking about it. If the brain had to analyze and process that situation (a car driving erratically) and then tell our body how to respond (swerve), it'd be too late. This "thinking without thinking" requires instant messaging coming from another source: the gut.

The gut has a sense of knowing that travels fast, through afferent vagal fibers to the brain, and doesn't require analytical breakdown and deliberation because, somehow, it just knows. (By the way, the vagus nerve is the main component of the parasympathetic nervous system, which is responsible for the rest-and-digest response that counteracts the sympathetic fight-or-flight response). Just think about all the nonverbal messages that the gut is responsible for transmitting to the brain, in addition to other sensations coming from the heart brain, liver, and lungs via the vagus nerve. We are "reflexively" responding to these messages 24-7.

New insights on the gut-brain connection are making a big impact on the understanding of the body-mind connection in medicine. Because of this, gastroenterologists are taking on the role of counselors to soothe an unsettled, anxiety-riddled gut. Also, companies like Viome and Wild Health are analyzing the gut's biome to ensure the bugs in the gut are optimized for better results in both the gut and brain. Not only is our diet impacting our thinking through the gut, but the sympathetic nervous system's stress response negatively impacts the gut causing irritable bowel symdrome

(IBS), constipation, inflammation, nausea, and other unsavory things. Improving one's diet, sleep, and exercise will greatly improve the gut's functioning, while activities such as meditation, breathwork, and yoga will downregulate the sympathetic fight-or-flight system. They do this by activating its parasympathetic sister through massaging the vagus nerve and calming the brain's activities (read excess thinking). These practices greatly increase resilience and propel us on an upward spiral of uncommon awesomeness. As a bonus we also develop increased awareness of how our bodies and minds function, upping our intuitional intelligence.

In the next section, we will explore the benefits of mastering inner and outer awareness to gain a deeper understanding of the gut, our oft-ignored second brain.

The science-y stuff for this chapter is done, by the way! (*You're welcome!*)

OUTER AND INNER AWARENESS

We can direct our attention in a focused manner on a single subject (or object), like a flashlight, or in an expansive manner on the context of your situation, like a scanner or floodlight. The former, let's call it *focused attention*, requires hard concentration on a singular thing. This is trained with concentration meditation using box breathing and/or mantra. The latter, let's call it *expansive attention*, requires mindful awareness on the totality, or context instead of content. This is trained with mindfulness meditation, long periods of

silence and extended time in nature, amongst other meth-
ods. Developing keen awareness of the context of our world
leads to greater intuitional skill. You can train your mind to
see more, and recognize more patterns, in the world around
you. This is handy for SEALs deep in enemy territory, and
for you as you engage in important decisions or negotiations.
The training requires that you learn to relax your focused
attention to allow for imprinting of the sensations and patterns that stream into your awareness. With some time, you
will develop greater sensitivity, or "situational awareness" to
your surroundings. The more you practice this skill, the more
readily you can sense an outlier—or any disruption—in your
environment. Mastering outer awareness aligns the brain and
gut to be in tune with the senses and sensations flowing into,
and from within, your body (inner awareness).

Apache scouts would fine-tune their awareness by reading the concentric rings in nature and noting the source
of the pattern at the center of the ring. That was where the
threat, or food, was. Recall when you tossed a stone into a
pond or skipped one across water. You watched as the water rippled out in rings until the waves could no longer be
detected. There are concentric rings like this in nature too.
Any change in the environment can be detected because it,
too, ripples out. The Apache scouts were so intuitive about
changes in their environment that they could track the intru-
sion of a single man eight miles away.

For instance, if a hunter scared a deer and it stepped into
the home of a fox, causing it to flee, the fox fleeing would cause
birds to take flight, which would cause another disturbance,

and on and on. . . . By sensing fear in a fox, hearing a bird squawk strangely, seeing a squirrel move erratically, Apache scouts could work their way backward to discern the original cause of the disruption and either avoid the danger or move toward the opportunity.

If you master the ability to read your surroundings like this, you will avoid all threats and thrive in any environment. It is not nearly as easy, however, to detect slight variations and concentric rings in the wilderness as it is in a still pond. Nonetheless, with practice, you will be able to tell when a hawk becomes agitated, a fox appears paranoid, or when a squirrel acts . . . well squirrely. And, just as the ripples in a pond will eventually wave back toward the source (the stone), being able to read the concentric rings in nature will bring you to the source of the disruption.

You can learn how to become attuned to the symphony of nature by spending time in it, or with the help of a course on nature survival or tracking such as Boulder Outdoor Survival School, National Outdoor Leadership School (NOLS), or Tom Brown Jr.'s Tracker School. Gaining an intuitive edge for survival and a deep understanding of the interconnectedness of all living things is invaluable and deeply rewarding.[4]

My SEAL teammates used these skills with great success in Iraq and Afghanistan. A SEAL platoon sent on a sniper operation to help the Marines clear Ramadi was led by my teammate Lieutenant Commander Jocko Willink. He and his men would go into the city and set up hide sites where they would sit quietly, just observing the whole of what was going on. They watched the rhythm and patterns of the city, developing situational awareness. This enabled them to detect anything out of place, or any disturbances like the Apache scouts did in a different wilderness.

If an individual acted in a contradictory pattern or stopped to peek around a corner or carried something that looked a little different while walking from the market, the SEALs made note. If a group of warrior-aged males clustered together and moved toward a common place or if someone took up a position on a roof, the SEAL team would react accordingly. Practicing this outer awareness kept them tuned in to the threats and opportunities to eliminate those threats. Jocko's team was so successful that the enemy knew him by name, similar to how the Vietcong knew of legendary SEAL Team Six founder Demo Dick Marcinko in Vietnam.

At SEAL Team Three, we trained to hone situational awareness relentlessly. We had drills where we would travel the same route over and over and try to observe more and more detail. We would slowly imprint the most minute details, and then any variances in those details on latter trips. This not only developed great intuitive awareness but also enhanced our memories.

But we had another drill for our memory, too, called a *KIM GAME* (KIM=Keep in Memory). We'd put twenty or more items under a blanket, then pull the blanket away and the SEAL had sixty seconds to memorize everything. The first time we might remember 50 percent of the items. But, over time, we'd learn to use our mind in different ways. We'd breathe into it, soften our gaze, and use expansive attention to open our minds to imprint, like taking a picture with a camera. We had to look at the whole field at once. The more we practiced, the more information would be there for us in greater and greater detail. If a watch was there, we could tell what time it was, memorize the make, etc. The details became that clear.

These examples reinforce the power of the brain to collect information beyond conscious awareness. But we cannot become masters of intuition until we also fine-tune inner awareness for what to pull from the memory banks of our unconscious minds.

This inner awareness is called *inferential intuition*. Unlike transrational intuition and women's intuition, inferential intuition pulls from life experiences or training as described above. Life experiences groove episodic memories that create a mental map in your hippocampus, located in the brain's temporal lobe.[5] Inferential intuition is built over a lifetime. Take a long-serving Navy SEAL, a veteran computer coder, or a master musician or athlete, for example. When they take action, they seem to operate out of instinct. Because their minds have mapped their trade or skill in so many ways that are not rote memory, but nonlinear and nonrational, they can spontaneously recognize new patterns for near-perfect unconscious solutions. Really, this is inferential intuition at work: Pattern recognition causes a solution to magically appear. It's coming out of them or through them. In this way, inferential intuition develops from long periods of practice. Conscious practice is what your brain does as it logs your life's events, turning a small fraction of them into memories. But this intuitive skill will assist in making present-moment assessments and decisions at a speed the conscious brain can't handle.

In the previous chapter, we learned that a message from our gut generally comes to us in the form of a sensation or hit that is felt, and rarely an internally cognized sound. But that can happen also, as when I felt (or heard internally) the word *stop*. And we learned that we are born with transrational intuition but lose it over time for lack of use or belief in it. We also practiced a listening body scan to get reacquainted with our bodies' natural intuitive senses. Using skills such as memory games to increase outer awareness of our surroundings helps heighten our inferential awareness too. These exercises work together.

Just as Apache scouts and SEAL snipers must be in tune with their surroundings so they can *infer* what's going to happen next, a pro athlete, linguist, dancer, chef, master sculptor, or any other creative vocation or activity uses inferential intuition too. The constant practice of one or a few skills required to master any profession, task, or activity (especially right-brained activities) creates deep-pattern synaptic grooving—neural pathways just like our fear loops and transformational loops.

You needn't have the archetype of a warrior or artist to possess these skills or master them. Think about other professions, such as teachers or merchants. How great would it be to anticipate the needs of your students or trust your gut during every business transaction?

HOLISTIC AWARENESS

When inner and outer awareness unite to create a heightened sense of intuition, I call this *holistic awareness*.

Having a heightened holistic awareness will alert you to the faintest intuitive signals in critical moments. Holistic awareness isn't a God-given gift. You must take deliberate steps to make holistic intuition part of your overall intelligence toolkit by developing your inner and outer awarenesses separately. If you don't, you're denying yourself the right to universal information and you're relying on hope and chance.

A superintendent at a local school put his intuitional intelligence to use to diffuse a potentially life-and-death situation. He was a student of my SEALFIT Kokoro program and had worked on these skills. One day a teacher called him saying a student in her class was wearing a military uniform and carrying a backpack, and it made her uncomfortable. My superintendent friend immediately thought that this was a pattern disrupt that signaled danger and told her to sit tight. Then, he called the sheriff, but didn't just leave it to them. He and another teacher darted to the room, surprising the student and physically removing him and his backpack. They escorted him into an isolated area where, sure enough, they found a weapon and ammo in his bag. There were more in the student's car. The teacher and the superintendent trusted their guts, and likely saved lives.

When you watch the patterns going on in your environment, it allows you to pay uncommon attention to any outliers and get an intuitive hit when you notice something off. This doesn't have to be life or death every time. A guy you work with may have suffered a recent loss. If your intuitional intelligence is on high alert, you will sense his pain and may be able to be a source of comfort, even if that means easing his workload. It doesn't mean you have to make him talk about what happened. Don't forget that when you follow your intuition's direction, other people's intuitive senses can pick up on that too. And that is often enough.

Common people don't take the time to master this skill. Instead of listening to their intuition, they have their heads down in their smartphones, absorbed in their own activities, bouncing their way through the day. Training your intuitive body-mind system will allow you to be much more open to what's going on with yourself, with those you love, and with others in any environment, whether familiar or foreign. You'll sense danger or opportunity and respond accordingly, while everyone else is still trying to figure out what's going on.

And here's another big reason to develop holistic awareness: to align with your ethos, you must trust your intuitive intelligence. You can't just rely on the biases of your rational mind or the stories people tell you. It's a huge source of inspiration and wisdom that most of us don't tap into. We are trained to think it would be irresponsible or strange to take orders from sensations over our rational mind.

That is one of many of the areas our society has gotten dead wrong.

YOUR ARCHETYPAL INTUITION

Listening to your surroundings and the messages from within doesn't just help you make strong decisions in sticky situations; it helps you find your purpose. It's a key component to developing and living an Uncommon Life.

When you look at a particular culture, you'll see that certain people fulfill specific roles within their society or community. When you pay attention to how these signals affect your actions and story, you'll get insight into how to move away from, or into, fulfilling specific roles to follow your *calling, or path*. Whether you're a warrior, a joker, healer, or monk, ask yourself: *Have you been forced into this role or is it instinctual?*

A clear example of an archetype that is forced on some of us is the role the firstborn child plays in the family dynamic. Now, many firstborn children are natural leaders with innate nurturing instincts. At the loss of one or both parents, these people are born leaders and natural caregivers, and it could well be their calling to take over the helm. However, not every firstborn child is destined for this role. I bet many of you are either nodding or shaking your heads, thinking about yourselves or a sibling that has had to take over the role of a parent. And I bet you just got a hit in your gut—notifying you if it's the right course for you or them or going against all the laws of nature.

We see this with teachers. Some are natural-born educators. Others are wildly intelligent but can't teach a puppy to heel with a piece of bacon in their pocket, and we wonder why they're in the profession when they'd make more effective scientists or engineers or authors.

Although you feel lucky when you trust your gut by accident, it's not just luck or chance. You're listening. Keep it up!

We must learn to trust our guts!

EXERCISE 12
Developing Inferential Intuition

Grab your journal and take a walk to a quiet place in nature. If you don't live in a place where lush surroundings or a beach are readily available, any outdoor place where you can feel safe and relaxed will do. FYI: this is a two-part sensory exercise— auditory and visual—to heighten your inferential awareness.

Start by box breathing for five or more minutes.

Part 1: Release all your other senses but your hearing, and just relax and listen to the sounds around you. Do this for five or ten minutes.

Next, take your journal and write down everything you can remember about what you heard in your surroundings.

Part 2: On your way back, when you're one or two blocks from home, look around and notice everything you can. On arriving at home, write it all down.

If you're a goal-oriented person like I am, performing these two exercises three or four times over the next week or so will allow to see progress. Inspiring!

Great work so far. We've gone over the difference between transrational and inferential intuition and gained a physiological understanding of the brain-gut connection and how all our reflexive decision-making comes from a signal that originates in the body and travels to the brain. We also learned about inner and outer awareness and how it's vital to train both skills to achieve holistic awareness.

In this third and final chapter of Mastering Your Intuitional Mountain, we will explore our heart intuition and the connection it has to everyone, and everything, around us.

And we will learn about mindfulness meditation and myriad other ways to develop our intuition.

13

HEART INTUITION

Scientists have long understood inferential intuition as a function of the unconscious mind, accessing existing information within the brain from forgotten experiences. In the early 2000s, Dr. Dean Radin of the Institute of Noetic Sciences designed a study to document the phenomena involving the perception of future information, and to understand the role the heart plays in receiving and relaying it.

The study used twenty-six participants, eleven males and fifteen females between the ages of eighteen and fifty-six. The participants were shown thirty calm and fifteen emotion-arousing color photos in randomized order over the course of two weeks.

Data from more than 2,300 trials were collected, measuring skin conductance, electroencephalogram (EEG) readings, from which cortical and heartbeat-evoked potentials were derived, and electrocardiogram (ECG) readings, from which cardiac decelerations/accelerations were derived.

These measures were used to investigate where and when in the brain and body intuitive information is processed. The electrophysiological data was recorded and registered prior to the visual stimulus in every instance.

The results determined that:

- The apprehension of information pertaining to future emotional events is a system-wide process involving the heart and the brain, and even the body as a whole.
- Informational input to the heart occurs about 4.75 seconds before the visual stimulus is presented . . . and then it travels to the brain via afferent vagal fibers, arriving about 1.3 seconds later.
- Once the pre-stimulus information is received, it appears to be processed in the same way as conventional sensory input.
- The bigger the emotion around the future event, the bigger the pre-stimulus hit to the heart.
- Women are more attuned to receiving this information than men based on more drastic changes in cortical levels and heartbeat variance. (This, we already know.)

Ultimately, the study presented compelling scientific evidence for the existence of transrational intuition. It further demonstrated that the body's perceptual apparatus is continuously scanning the future.[1]

Our intuition is turned on! It's just waiting for us to put it to good use.

Now, let me ask you this: Can you imagine turning on your lawn mower and then going inside to binge your favorite show? Turning on your car and then going for a walk? Turning on the blender and then going to take a shower? I could go on and on with this one. My point is that people would think you were nuts if they saw you do any of that. Yet so many of us let our intuition idle in place, all the while it's itching to go for a spin.

In this chapter, we will explore our heart intuition to better understand its vast, universal power over all our relationships and every facet of our life and life purpose. And I will teach you the sure-fire way that everyone can master their intuitive intelligence.

THE HEART OF THE MATTER

Oxytocin is produced in the hypothalamus, which is a region located at the base of the brain. The hypothalamus serves as a control center for various physiological processes and plays a crucial role in regulating emotions. After its production in the hypothalamus, oxytocin is then released from the posterior pituitary gland, which is connected to the hypothalamus via a structure known as the pituitary stalk. From there, oxytocin enters the bloodstream and exerts its effects on various target tissues and organs throughout the body, particularly the heart. Research suggests that oxytocin plays a role in promoting feelings of bonding, trust, and social connection, and it has often been referred to as the *love hormone* or *bonding hormone.*

Studies have shown that oxytocin will also positively influence cardiovascular function. When oxytocin is released into the bloodstream, it can have vasodilatory effects, which means it can help widen blood vessels, leading to decreased blood pressure. This effect is thought to be related to the hormone's role in promoting social bonding and reducing stress. Moreover, oxytocin can also have cardioprotective effects. Some research indicates that oxytocin may help reduce inflammation in the cardiovascular system and protect the heart from certain types of damage. It has been suggested that oxytocin's ability to reduce stress and anxiety may contribute to its positive impact on heart health. Its role in cardiovascular function is still an area of ongoing research, and more studies are needed to fully understand the extent of its effects on the heart and overall cardiovascular health.

We can use this knowledge to actively promote the release of oxytocin for more heart-centered awareness. Develop sensitivity to the heart's intuition by placing your attention into your heart region, both by visualizing your heart opening, and focusing your inner awareness on what the heart feels like. When you do this, your heart intuition will be on full alert when communicating authentically with an individual, with a team, or to a large group in a leadership capacity. *Hormones and Behavior* published an article in June of 2017 proving that the release of oxytocin promotes group bonding and cooperation at a higher level no matter how cognitively challenging the task and regardless of gender.[2]

To speak from your heart space and open your heart's intuition, breathe deeply and imagine your consciousness dropping into the heart region, thereby expanding it, before you begin communicating. With this practice you will not only communicate with more authenticity, but your listening skills will also be heightened.

Sounds easy enough, right? Certainly, anyone can perform these simple steps.

So, why don't we?

Most of us try to live honest lives and do unto others. But have you ever stopped to notice that we also tend to express ourselves in ways that are ineffective, with words that dance somewhere above the actual truth of the matter? We speak from our heads all day every day with our defenses up.

Here are some scenarios of tough life situations that could benefit from paying attention to the voice in our heart:

Jackson is a high schooler who gets good grades, plays sports, and has a part-time job. But despite getting adequate sleep, Jackson is always tired. His parents fight incessantly over his "laziness." They blame genetics, squabbling over whose side of the family is lazier. They blame lack of sun. They blame marijuana, though Jackson is drug-free. (They test him monthly.) The problem? Jackson's mom has issues with alcohol, and it's stressed him to the max. And Jackson's dad, rather than facing this, keeps playing the what-could-be-wrong-with-Jackson game with Mom. Meanwhile, the truth of the matter stays buried deep inside the family chest, as all the ineffective, analytical, left-brained words exchanged between his parents dance on top of it.

John has anger issues. He's from a hotheaded Italian family. This is his excuse. John, however, hates his mid-level job at a big construction firm and wants to start his own company, building tiny homes. But he doesn't discuss this truth with his wife, Rebecca. He just wakes up angry Monday through Friday, while she tiptoes around his moods. They're one bad argument away from filing for divorce. What's worse is John doesn't even know that starting his own business would solve all this. It's never occurred to him to listen to his heart.

Renée is applying to med schools. Though she wants to write the next great American novel, she's afraid to tell anyone. So, she keeps living the lie because she's got a mind for math and science.

Kyler could be a starter at a D3 school, playing basketball. His parents, siblings, and friends are pushing him in that direction. He commits to the small school, though his heart keeps telling him to walk onto his D1 dream team and tough it out. Kyler no longer sleeps well at night since he signed his life away.

These are pretty typical examples of situations in which we find ourselves or people we know. You get one, two, three, or more people together—with no one using their heart intuition as a guide—and you've got a breeding ground for issues that can really kick you and your loved ones in the collective pants, again and again. You can go through your whole life never speaking "from the heart." When Thoreau said *"the mass of men lead lives of quiet desperation,"* he was referring to this. And this happens on grand scales, too, with leaders and countries. It can and is happening on the world stage. Not listening to your heart's intuition is common, it's the norm, it's what "the mass of men" do.

Listening to your heart's voice and speaking that truth is for the practiced and the brave.

You must learn to be present and open your heart to achieve this level of authenticity.

This practice takes courage, just as having a conversation about alcoholism takes courage. And switching careers takes courage. And walking onto your dream team, knowing you won't be a starter, takes an assload of courage. Listening to your intuition builds emotional resilience and strong relationships because that voice is honest and coming from a place of pure love: your heart.

When I sat on the bench with Nakamura, heart feelings arose that I wasn't prepared for—like realizing I was extremely unhappy in my current career, and that when I saw myself twenty years into the future working for my father's company, I became nauseated and lethargic. My heart sank whenever that image came to mind. But I was thankful for the insight, the sick feeling in my heart, and the energy zap. I had tapped into my truth for the first time ever, and I was finally paying attention. Intuitively, I knew that I would not bring my best self to that future.

It was a start. I could then ask the question: *What other possible futures exist?* That's when I started to get insights and a direct knowing. I saw a warrior and leader who was happy and healthy two decades down the road. This image would arise without much work after I initially tapped into it. I had shoveled the dirt out from on top of my treasure chest of truth (to stick with that analogy). *Now to tell my parents . . .*

There's a name for this type of meditation, when you still your mind and focus on your inner surroundings, what you're sensing and feeling in the moment. . . .

MASTERING PRESENT-MOMENT AWARENESS

Mindfulness meditation is an excellent form of sensory awareness training. It connects your head to the insights your heart and gut are sending—where realizations or solutions to complex, nonrational problems reside. You tap into these intuitive signals by asking good questions when you're in a deep state of presence. In fact, one of the most powerful tools we have at our disposal for receiving insight and direct knowingness is mindfulness meditation.

This is where the truth lives.

The next time you're dealing with an issue that you don't have a solution for, try mindfulness meditation to get to the root of it. Don't worry about solving the problem. Just focus on understanding how the problem arose in the first place. This is the part we naturally overlook: the truth of the matter! And we don't just overlook it because we don't want to face our role in the latest of life's hurdles we must now leap, but our brains, as you know, are wired to seek solutions. Plus, our brains are more naturally wired to solve problems than they are to go back in time and dissect the cause (and our role in it). Yes, we dwell on the past; boy, do we ever. That is not the same as backtracking to gain an understanding of why a problem occurred in the first place.

But that is what we must do: go back to the source.

Thinking back to the source is the direct link to the solution. It's actually a shortcut! And not just that but understanding how the problem started in the first place will prevent you from doing it again. We must become scouts, finding the source of our issues, for therein lies our truth. Practicing mindfulness doesn't just get to the heart of life's issues, it trains us to be present and attuned to the voice in our heart.

With mindfulness meditation, you use expansive attention to simply observe the things happening in your body-mind system. You let go of attachment, judgment, latching onto a thought pattern, and riding it to its natural conclusion. You're in an open and expansive state of mind, which is the opposite of how our mind works when we think.

When we think, we use focused attention, which narrows our attention and is often accompanied by a furrowing of the eyebrows. This expends energy. Take a moment to think about that Rubik's Cube. (If it wasn't, I bet your brow is furrowed now!) Thinking attaches you to a thought. It's a specific process. Can you see how this is different than mindfulness meditation? It's different from concentration exercises too. During box breathing or the Zen counting practice, we focus on numbers, which moves us away from our thoughts to focus on counting.

In mindfulness meditation, you relax into receiving information. You're just watching passsively. Your witness is observing. If something comes up, great. If not, great. Let it go. You're a mountain watching the clouds drift by. But if you start thinking, you become one of the clouds, and you move wherever it goes. But you are not the cloud. You are not headed east or wherever. You are simply being. You want to develop a more spacious mind. This is how you do it, by being the mountain.

Our intuition doesn't lie. It's incapable of it. If you use whole mind thinking in everything you do, you will receive insight from your heart-mind-gut, and that's the wisdom you will convey with your words. Once you start speaking from this level of knowing, it's impossible to dance over the truth. This skill is especially useful during challenging times. People are more receptive to this kind of truth, as science is proving. They recognize (often intuitively themselves) that it's coming from a place of kindness, from the heart.

Mastering intuitive intelligence, however, doesn't make you vomit truisms involuntarily once the bright-white spotlight of awareness blanches your face. During uncomfortable situations, we want to escape, default to the easiest way out. Men, especially, have a knack for avoiding tough conversations. *(C'mon, guys, you know it's true.)* The difference is you will know you're doing it once you begin to climb the mountain of intuitive intelligence. But, through practice, you will become hyperaware of what's really going on in every situation, both inside and outside yourself, and with others. The subtext will blare in your ears, even when words aren't one of the signals. This will make it harder and harder to avoid using your intuitive skills to speak the truth.

Once you're able to stabilize your mind on one thing through concentration practices and mindfulness meditation, you will naturally (*intuitively*) start practicing mindfulness throughout your day. This is how you will start moving past issues with greater ease. Over time, others will notice this innate wisdom you seem to possess. And you'll become a confidant and someone who people can trust. You'll become uncommon.

To train your intuition you must trust that your perceiving mind wants to help you. If you're always in the rational/linear, left-brained/thinking mind, you're always striving and grasping at knowledge. The intuitive, perceiving mind patiently waits, seeking understanding and trusting it will come. It is an open hand waiting to receive inspiration or intuitive signals from that future all-knowing source. Focused thinking (problem-solving and ruminating) takes energy to force results. Intuitive expansive thinking takes surrender to the intelligence that's in you or wants to come through you. And this, by the way, conserves energy, as we are merely observing the clouds as they pass by.

Be aware that when you start paying attention to your intuition for the very first time, you might think everything is a sign. You could toss on two different shoes one frazzled morning and decide it's your intuition telling you not to walk anywhere that day. Don't let yourself go batty or get hung up as you develop this new sense. Have a sense of humor about it! Putting on two different shoes is funny, especially if you don't realize it until you get to work or the gym. Relax. What the shoe thing was probably trying to tell you is you need to slow down and breathe. (Box breathe for even two minutes to reset your morning!)

A word of caution: our intuition can be hijacked by prejudice and social conditioning. Our intuitive senses are sensitive! They can also get overwhelmed by excessive sensory stimulation and information overload—and to say that is a giant problem in our techno-driven, media-flooded world is an understatement.[3]

If you pay attention, you'll realize the voice or message from your heart's intuition has a neutral tone to it, almost emotionless. It's simply passing on information. Paranoia comes from negativity and distrust—aberrant beliefs from your monkey mind, and there is generally a tone of anger or judgment and a feeling of fear or shame that accompanies the sensation.[4]

GROW YOUR INTUITIVE TOOLKIT

As you can guess, we'll be doing a mindfulness meditation for our final exercise. But there is a menagerie of ways to open your heart's intuition. If you haven't mastered an art or have any hobbies that wake up your right brain, picking one up and practicing it will help develop your intuitive intelligence. Martial arts engage the right brain. Movement arts, musical arts, vocal arts, visual arts, literary arts, language arts—these are all effective ways to unlock the intuitive areas of your heart-mind-gut. As you refine your skills, you'll access more genius during practice and performance.

Another way to expand your heart and deepen your intuitive neural pathways is through sensory awareness training and sensory deprivation training.

With sensory deprivation training, you deliberately shut off all your senses, like in a sensory deprivation chamber. You're in complete silence, floating in water and Epsom salts. It's dark. You feel weightless. With no other signals, you can focus all your attention on your inner world: your thoughts and sensations. You'll become more sensitive to the signals your heart, brain, gut, or other parts of your body give you in the form of an image or a direct knowingness.

But don't get carried away with this if you decide to try it! Sitcoms such as *The Simpsons, Modern Family,* and *The Big Bang Theory* all did episodes poking fun at deprivation chambers. Though hilarious, once the humor fizzled out, the characters in the chambers discovered a truth about themselves that was buried beneath their conscious mind.

If none of these are your thing, you can master your intuitional mountain through good, old-fashioned meditative practices.

INTUITIVE INTERCONNECTEDNESS

As you practice connecting at a deeper level with your heart, you'll experience more presence with others. You'll feel their feelings and be able to ask better questions. You'll be upping your intuitional awareness to levels on par with intuitive empaths—but without all the baggage! You will be outside yourself and feeling into others at will. When you're in a day-to-day situation, you'll enter each environment with a deep state of awareness to the patterns around you, to how people are behaving, and to individual and group moods and attitudes. Approaching life in this way, you'll notice anything that seems off and recognize it well in advance of your peers (another empathic quality) because you will be attuned to your transrational and inferential intuition.

If you go into a room and feel that something's off in your heart and belly, you won't barrel into problem-solving mode. You'll take your time. Then you'll move into authentic listening mode. You'll develop a much deeper heart level connection with that (those) individual(s), and you'll be a conduit for clearing the air. You'll also have much more effective interactions with coworkers. You'll find yourself and your team identifying and solving problems at a much deeper level than before, and at a much quicker pace. You'll deepen relationships with family members. (And who doesn't need to do that with at least one member of their nuclear family?) If you have a partner in life, you won't believe what this skill will do to transform your relationship to euphoric levels of happiness and harmony.

According to Steve Jobs, intuition is "*more powerful than intellect.*" It's "*one of the four major functions of the brain*" as was determined by Carl Jung. And it's considered "*the only valuable thing we have at our disposal*" in Albert Einstein's estimation.

EXERCISE 13
Mindfulness Meditation

Journaling strengthens pattern recognition. Let's combine this with mindfulness meditation.

Start with a concentration practice, such as box breathing, and drop into your witness.

Then, after five or so minutes, let's begin a mindfulness meditation practice.

Breathe deeply and imagine your consciousness dropping into the heart region and expanding it. Surrender to the experience.

After you become the mountain watching the thought-clouds pass by, start journaling what comes up. Do this for the next ten to twenty minutes. This will help you become more sensitive to what's going on in your inner mind and with your emotions.

Nice work.

So, what came up? What patterns did you notice? How do some of the thoughts you wrote down make you feel as you revisit them? Pay attention to how your heart and gut feels when you answer these questions.

Once you become comfortable with this practice, you can get even more specific, as I did when I studied with Nakamura.

- If there's an issue, reach out to your inferential intuition in the form of a question and free your mind, preparing yourself for whatever sensation or answer arises.
- If you're interested in receiving transrational information, set a positive intention, ask your question or for guidance, and settle into silence to free your mind and become the mountain.

The more you practice, the more information you will receive from your consciousness. This will start to feel like a structure of support under your feet. One message supports and complements the other and so on. Before long (even as little as eight weeks into this regular practice), you will feel the new and improved you, the authentic you, dusting off the dirt and moving beyond the surface of your subconscious.

And then, on emergence, you will begin to understand and fine-tune your powers of intuition in an exponential fashion.

The Japanese call this level of mastery *shibumi.* That means effortless perfection. It flows out of the deep patterning (the new neural pathways you've built), and it allows you to have razor-sharp intuition without active thought. You surrender into the awareness that your body-mind knows how to do this. You trust it. And you simply act out of it. You have cultivated wisdom.

BONUS EXERCISE 3
Gut Check!

Just as you gauged your thoughts from the mindfulness meditation practice, you can gut check people. Pick two or three people in your life right now and try it. Note how fast a feeling/sensation arises on the heels of the name that enters your brain. This information travels twice as fast as the speed of light, according to William A. Tiller's Theory of Wave Information Transmission.[5] In nonscientific terms, this exercise takes about two seconds! And the information it relays can be invaluable. You know what all that means? No excuses. But be prepared to surrender to whatever feelings surface.

Congrats! You've made it over the intuitional mountain. . . .

MASTERING YOUR INTUITIONAL MOUNTAIN
IN REVIEW

- We learned what a gut instinct is and how to recognize the signals or sensations when receiving messages from our intuition.
- We gained a deeper understanding of transrational and inferential intuition, outer and inner awareness,

and practiced a listening body scan to become more familiar with sensations in our bodies.

- We gained a scientific understanding of why our gut is considered the second brain, and how the gut and mind are interconnected.

- We studied the important role the heart plays—the heart intuition—in the decision-making process and when interacting with others. We broke down mindfulness meditation to understand the importance of surrendering to the all-knowing consciousness, which is where the unbiased truth resides. We discovered other ways we can up our intuitional awareness through right-brained activities.

In Part V: Mastering Your Spiritual Mountain, I will help you further develop the bulletproof plan you're imagining and preparing for in your mind. And I will remind you that you are on your way to laser-like focus and resiliency, through good times and bad by reviewing your progress. You are an unbeatable force that's in motion toward your destiny.

Part V

MASTERING YOUR SPIRITUAL MOUNTAIN

- We're going to revisit our *svadharma*, reason for being, and review reasons why we could miss our target mission. I'll introduce you to the Japanese *ikigai* chart to aid you in zeroing in on your path, and to eight virtue couplets that, when followed, create balance and resilience on your path to mastery.

- We're going to be reminded of my mentor's "one, day, one life" philosophy, which allows us to live mindfully with present-moment awareness. I will reinforce the importance of first thoughts, words, and actions, and last actions, words, and thoughts. We will review our progress since we began this journey and let go to flow.

- Finally, I will introduce you to the art of sacred silence to achieve spiritual mastery.

14

LIVE LIFE VIRTUOUSLY

*"What could be more futile, more insane, than to
create inner resistance to what already is? What could
be more insane than to oppose life itself?"*
—ECKHART TOLLE

The Japanese view the heart as the essential organ of life
and the source from which all action should emanate.
Their term for this alignment, *kokoro,* describes a person's way of being. It means "heart and mind aligned in action."
When aligned, there is less resistance to things as they are, leading to the state of acceptance—as Tolle describes. There isn't
one word in English to capture this essential nature.[1] Most believe the mind as the be-all and end-all. I think as we evolve in
our understanding of the body-mind-heart connection in the
Western world, we use the word *energy* more and more like the
Japanese do *kokoro.* "She has good energy" or "I don't like their
energy," we say. Also the word *spirit* is thrown into the mix,

which somewhat embodies what *kokoro* means because it's really about a person's essence: how they feel, think, and communicate when operating from their higher Self, with aligned body language, words, and actions.

Without realizing it (or maybe you do!), you have been developing your *kokoro* intelligence by climbing the other four mountains with this work we have been doing. Their integration creates mastery at the fifth mountain "*kokoro*-spirit" level. With your physical, mental, emotional, and intuitional intelligences all working together as a team, your blockages don't stand a chance. You are becoming limitless. You are acting from your whole mind, like the Zen-enlightened master. This mind, according to the great Zen teacher Suzuki Roshi, is a universal "Beginner's Mind," which is always on your side because a Zen mind is on the side of truth. It's the "mind" that just knows what is real, and what is not.

And when you have strong *kokoro,* you will know your *calling,* your *why.* It will reveal itself to you. If you're still unsure at this point, no worries. Stay the course! Give it a little more time, remain focused, and you'll get there.

In Part V: Mastering Your Spiritual Mountain, the final section in the book, we're going discover just how the five mountains of intelligence unify to create self-mastery.

YOUR REASON FOR BEING

When I told you about my adventures in business school back when I was in NYC, I left out a few details. I didn't tell you how hard it was to get my CPA certificate. I clawed my way through that program. It took me four attempts to pass the exam. Four! This should have been a sign. Thank goodness I was diligent in my meditative practice with Nakamura, which revealed my warrior archetype and unique *calling*, which led me to the SEALs. It was the right way for me to serve the world at that point in my life. Once there, all my limitations fell away. Life felt easy. In truth, I'd rather go back and do SEAL training all over again than sit through another CPA exam. It never felt right, and it never got easier because it wasn't my path. At no point did I intuitively feel in sync with accounting.

It's important to understand that your call of duty will most likely change throughout your life. Circumstances change constantly. You could be on a very clear path in your twenties that shifts in your mid-thirties. It may feel like it doesn't fit anymore, and you won't understand why. If you don't recognize that change in your calling, that the target has shifted, you could stay in something for too long and then move away from your *unique calling* again. Or now that you've committed to mastering the five levels of consciousness, maybe you feel confused again. This makes sense! Developing awareness does this.

I began to get hits about a different calling, a new direction, about the warrior calling my archetype was yearning for. And I had to take another leap of faith to figure out my next duty station in the world. As I mentioned earlier, I've begun to get a new hit about a more spiritual path, and I'm taking those steps currently.

As long as you're living, you have a duty to fulfill. It will be different in your twenties than in your thirties, forties, fifties, and so on. It will continue changing into your eighties and nineties. It changes because it's meant to be an intersection between your personal ethos, what the world wants and needs, and the vocation that's right for you given all the circumstances.

The Japanese use the concept of *ikigai* to map their life path. Loosely translated as a "reason for being," the concept narrows in on your calling. Back in the Mental Mountain section, we reduced the search by discovering our archetype(s) and creating a Likes List and a Dislikes List. This chart will take that exploration to the next level.

IKIGAI

生き甲斐

You love

PASSION · MISSION

Good at · IKIGAI · World needs

JOB · VOCATION

Paid for

Studying the *ikigai* chart makes it seem so easy, doesn't it? There are four areas of interest to consider when embarking on your purpose: *what you love, what you're good at, what the world needs,* and *what you can be paid for.* Where those intersect, you can narrow in on your passion, mission, vocation, and job, which converge to a center point. Your target is *what the world needs* and *what you can be paid for*—but it must align with your passion, purpose, and principles. It's critical to get this right because if you're not on the bull's-eye you'll feel discontent. And I want you happy as a clam at high water as you fulfill your mission!

You must hit the bull's-eye.

This is not as easy as it sounds. Here are some ways you could miss your path. You might:

- **Have poor aim**. You do something inspiring that doesn't align with your stand. Or you do something you stand for that doesn't pay the bills. You could aspire to be the best jet pack rider in the world, but you could have trouble making money that way today. When I was thirty, I thought that maybe I could be an astronaut, because I had some SEAL friends that went in that direction. Protocol was ten more years of education and experience. It wasn't my *calling,* even though it inspired me. It didn't fit. My aim would have been off.

- **Deny it.** You know your path but deny it to please others (usually your parents). You love playing the cello. Maybe you're even a prodigy. But your parents say, "Be serious, get practical. Do something that will earn a living."

- **Quit, due to grandiosity or low self-esteem**. You choose the right target, but your path exceeds your actual capacity. You want to be an entrepreneur and serve the world. You tell yourself, "I'm supposed to start the next Uber and make billions." So, you try it, it flops, and you retreat. You missed by overshooting or not getting the right schooling. Start by striving to become a GM at a local company. Conversely, you could have the skills but lack confidence and have negative inner dialogue. This is where meditation, positive self-talk, recapitulation, rewriting your story, and mindfulness meditation with an intention can serve you like nothing else.

- **Close yourself off to your true path.** This is where human inertia comes into play. You stay planted in your current career because of benefits, even though you're neither happy nor fulfilled. You become the walking dead, just marking time. You stay in the military for the last ten years, just to get the retirement package. You could be a financial services professional earning $600k annually, afraid to chase your dream of being an artist. Sometimes, age plays a role in inhibiting forward motion. There are so many examples of people in their sixties, seventies, and eighties who changed their state. Nelson Mandela was seventy-two when he was released from prison and seventy-six when he became president. Colonel Sanders first started franchising Kentucky Fried Chicken when he was sixty-five. If you're not dead, doing something new is not impossible. And if you're not near-dead, what are you waiting for?

THE PATH TO SELF-MASTERY

Self-mastery and staying on course toward your mission requires continual self-assessment and self-awareness. You can use a guide like this book to check your progress and get inspiration. (Start from the beginning once you get to the end!) I have read all my favorite books more than once. Tony Robbins, arguably the world's most famous life coach, said he's read *As a Man Thinketh* by James Allen more than a dozen times. I've read Napoleon Hill's *Think and Grow Rich* about that many times. I have also read spiritual texts, the Bible, the Bhagavad Gita, and the Yoga Sutras of Patanjali many times. You can also emulate the actions of people who inspire you, who've lived in a manner aligned with your vision—Nelson Mandela, Gandhi, Jesus, Buddha, Mother Teresa, Malala Yousafzai, or any hero you know. If you stop to notice, they're everywhere. They're on the front lines as soldiers in wartime and as EMTs, nurses, and doctors throughout the pandemic. They're teaching your kids and starting nonprofits to fight racism, male-on-female violence, and illiteracy. Some of these heroes are kids who've found their *calling* early and started lemonade stands to fight cancer, or have donated their allowances to buy food for the homeless as in the case of young Austin Perine and his Show Love Foundation.

Staying on target with your unique calling means mastering the following virtues. I've coupled them into soft and hard virtues, kind of like yin and yang, where yin is inner: reflection, potential, feminine, flowing; and yang is outer: action, performance, masculine, rigid. When you find balance, each of these couplets becomes an infinity loop, flowing back and forth unrestricted. Part of the *kokoro* mindset is to appreciate the flow instead of struggling between being one way or the other on one end of the polarity spectrum.

- **Simplicity and Boldness:** When you develop a plan, your brain will try to be clever and make things more complex than they need to be. Steve Jobs was a great proponent of simplicity in Apple's products. But take your simple plan and be bold. Elon Musk has a clear and simple vision for his companies but backs it by an extraordinarily bold attitude and approach. That's a warrior virtue. (FYI: I'm using "warrior" as a general moniker here and not referring to an archetype.)

- **Excellence and Non-Attachment:** A warrior strives for excellence. "Day by day, I'm getting better and better." That's the warrior's mantra. As James Clear recommends in his international bestseller, *Atomic Habits,* you want to strive for consistent improvements of 1 percent daily. The soft side of this mindset is non-attachment to your achievements. Enjoy the journey. Non-attachment leads to humility.

- **Drive and Contentment:** The warrior is driven to master their craft. But often, people with drive are malcontents. Author, entrepreneur, and strategic coach Dan Sullivan says in *The Gap and the Gain* that people who are malcontent haven't navigated the gap properly. You should be measuring your progress against where you

started, not where you want to go. The progress gap fu-
els you with momentum, energy, and confidence.

- **Trust and Respect:** Trust is an action. You act out of trust
  to demonstrate you possess this quality. And the more
  you respect yourself, the more others respect you, the
  more trustworthy you become. At the partner or team
  levels, this becomes a virtuous loop, too, cementing a
  bond that bolsters everyone's spirit and performance.

- **Justice and Peace:** You extend your hand in peace, but if
  someone does something evil in response, you can easily
  close that hand into a fist. The great Apaches said that
  the true warrior is the last to pick up a lance, but he's
  willing to do so and lay down his life for others to bring
  justice. Often, people take no action to take a stand. This
  method doesn't always work. Cultivate peace, but not to
  the extent that you let someone trample you.

- **Courage and Commitment:** When you act with courage, it reinforces your commitment to your mission or
  team. It requires courage to leave a bad situation, but it
  allows you to commit to something better. As a leader
  of the SEALs, four-star Admiral Bill McRaven committed ten years to getting Osama bin Laden. His courage-
  commitment loop was unbreakable, and it led to bin
  Laden's demise.

- **Honor and Truth:** Honor is seen in action, which
  comes from directives from your heart intuition, where
  the soft, unbiased truth lives. When I was in Iraq, in
  2004, my commanding officer, Captain O'Connell,

used to say: *"If you're going to take an action and are uncertain, how would you want to read about this if it showed up in* The New York Times *on Monday?"* This test will determine whether your behavior is honorable.

• **Discipline and Joy:** Challenge yourself daily to improve, exercise, eat well, sleep well, and speak well. Warriors are disciplined. The challenge of being disciplined, however, goes away with time. That's the soft side of discipline—joy. Bestselling author and my teammate from SEAL Team 3, Jocko Willink, will tell you in his bestseller, *Extreme Ownership,* that discipline equals freedom. I really like that. Without discipline, you're a slave to your lack of ability.

If you don't feel as if you're on the full *kokoro* path yet, at least keep it at a slow burn in your life. Self-assess periodically and contemplate on the eight virtue loops. Step into your possible archetypes every day until you figure out your next calling. It's better to dive in daily than hope to develop the skills when things fall apart. Otherwise, you'll be discontent, unfulfilled, and not able to perform at your peak along the way. It will lead to a crisis of confidence. You won't be able to see your future clearly. You'll feel like you're drifting, dying inside, giving up, being left behind, or missing your calling with no mission focus. One or more of those reasons may be why you were drawn to *Uncommon* in the first place. So, don't stop now. We've come so far!

EXERCISE 14
Ikigai Chart

As your journey of integration continues up the five mountains, it's important to check in with your foundational ethos. Whether you've narrowed down your archetype and *svadharma* or not, take a few minutes to create your own *ikigai* chart.

Start with five or more minutes of box breathing to calm your mind before filling in the chart.

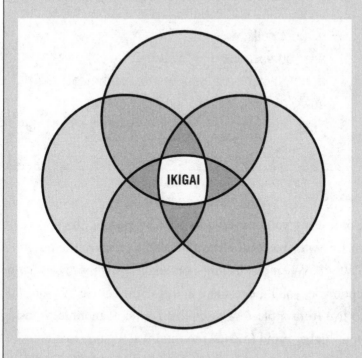

Now, use the chart to assist in answering the questions below. And, if you need to, take a look back at your Likes List and Dislikes List, and what you wrote for your possible archetypes.

1. How does the chart inform your sense of self?
2. Are you, in general, living the Uncommon Life meant for you?
3. Are you on the right path?
4. Are you hitting the center of your *kokoro* target?
5. Are you mastering yourself using universal principles that guide behavior and align with your highest self?
6. Are you virtuous in all you do?
7. If not, where are you out of alignment? Write down the virtues you need to work on.
8. Then make a plan to get yourself back to the bull's-eye.

Connecting your training to your purpose is the motivator. In this way, you will always be able to answer the question: "Why?" When bad things or challenging obstacles come upon you, you'll be resilient and stay the course. As you start to live from a place of discipline (physical mountain), using your higher mind (mental mountain) as a guide that takes instructions from your heart and gut (emotional and intuitional mountains), this is what it means to have strong *kokoro*.

In the final chapter, we're going to review the importance of first thoughts, last thoughts, and present-moment awareness. "As a man thinketh in his heart, so is he."—Proverbs 23:7.

15

ONE DAY, ONE LIFE

I f you're familiar with some of my other work, you know that "one day, one lifetime" is part of the foundational philosophy of my teacher, Kaicho Nakamura. Today is your first day. Today may be your only day. So, above all, make it your best day. And do this every day. There is no reason to obsess about things that could go wrong or about people who may hurt you. In this one day you have, there's no time to dwell in victimhood. This is it. You only have today.

Your conscious, awakened life is simply a series of moments strung together. Your conditioned mind separates those moments into past, present, and future. It's your job to learn to be connected to the present. This is the moment that matters. In doing so, you will enter into a state of flow and cultivate deep awareness. All the power you possess will be available to flow through you. And this is how you approach your *One Day*, the only day you really have right now.

If you ascribe to this philosophy, waking up in the morning is like birth. You open your eyes, your mind regains conscious awareness, and you are born again into this beautiful world (or better, this beautiful world is born to you again). By the same token, the last thought you have and final breath you take before falling into a deep sleep is the metaphorical death of your day. This is your opportunity to clear the slate should you be blessed to live another day. Be thoughtful and precise with how you start and end your One Day for, when strung together, these days create your Uncommon Life.

In the morning, take responsibility for your first thoughts, first words, and then first actions. Use your mantra. Every day. Before you know it, this will become involuntary.

At the end of the day, take responsibility in reverse order— for your last actions, words, and thoughts before you drift off to sleep. Be deliberate with your thoughts. They're critically important. They can determine how well you sleep and affect your mood on rising.

In this way, every day is a mini encapsulation of a lifetime bracketed by your first thoughts, words, and actions and last thoughts, words, and actions.

FIRST THOUGHTS, WORDS, AND ACTIONS

Have you heard of William Edwards Deming? Born in 1900, he was an American statistician who first became famous for his reconstruction efforts in Japan's economy in post-WWII, shooting many of their companies, such as Toyota and Sony, to number one status in the global economy with his fourteen-point theory on Total Quality Management. It would be decades before companies like Ford would surrender to a growth mindset and retain his services. America's reluctance to embrace the Deming System of Profound Knowledge and incorporate it into their business practices is one of the reasons *U.S. News & World Report* has referred to him as one of the "nine hidden turning points in history."[1]

One of his main themes was the importance of getting the beginning of any venture right: *"By focusing on the first 15 percent of anything, the remaining 85 percent will effortlessly follow."* **It stands to reason that if you place quality focus on your first thoughts, first words, and first actions, the rest of the day will take care of itself . . . all the way through to your last actions, words, and thoughts. But you must be consistent.**

Your morning mantra is critical to the rest of your day.

My first thoughts are: *I like myself. I love myself. I am whole, worthy, and competent.* Then, I add: *Wake up and be awesome! I've got another chance to do this well, to learn more, and be better. I got this, easy day, hooyah!* What all this says to my spirit and my ego is that I'm in charge of this day. I could stop there, but those are all "I" statements. So, I go to my higher self with gratitude. I think about my Creator and offer my service and actions up to that power. With my Christian upbringing, one of the ways that I do this is to recite the "Peace Prayer of St. Francis of Assisi."

Lord, make me an instrument of your peace.
Where there is hatred, let me bring love.
Where there is offense, let me bring pardon.
Where there is discord, let me bring union.
Where there is error, let me bring truth.
Where there is doubt, let me bring faith.
Where there is despair, let me bring hope.
Where there is darkness, let me bring your light.
Where there is sadness, let me bring joy.
O Master, let me not seek as much
To be consoled as to console,
To be understood as to understand,
To be loved as to love.
For it is in giving that one receives,
It is in self-denying that one finds,
It is in pardoning that one is pardoned,
It is in dying that one is raised to eternal life.

That takes my first thoughts from me, Mark Divine, and connects them to my higher self and higher power. I become aware of my body with consciousness. I move from my body to my mind and then to my spirit. I lead with my first thought back to Source, back to God. In this way, I feel reborn.

I follow my morning ritual, connecting my thoughts to my ethos, my vision for the future, my mission, and my targets for the day. I link everything so I'm very clear on where I'm going with my life by the time I am done with the ritual. Then I'm ready to get busy, kicking ass and taking names.

When you wake up, the first words in your mind are

naturally to yourself. But, before long, you will start speaking, maybe to your dog, spouse, kids, coworkers. This practice helps you be more mindful, so that your first words to others are positive, helpful, and connecting. My first words to my wife, Sandy, are usually: "Wake up, and be awesome, babe!" As an add-on, we express words of gratitude to each other. It's a wonderful practice for couples.

Only you can be responsible for the quality of your first thoughts and words and how they land. So make sure they're powerful, positive, productive, and coming from a place of love—the other 85 percent of your day depends on it!

Georgetown professor and *New York Times* bestselling author Cal Newport coined the term *deep work* in his book by the same name. I love that term, as it describes what I'd like to see happen after your morning ritual.

After your mantra and words of gratitude, after you check in with your ethos and your mission and priority targets, Newport says that your first action should be to accomplish the hardest or most important thing with all your effort. That's doing the deep work first. We're talking about thirty to ninety minutes of uninterrupted, concentrated effort on a mission-oriented task—before you check your email, hop on a phone call, or start a meeting. Newport theorizes that doing this will render massive benefits in your life.[2]

You might say, "Yeah, but my first conference call is at seven a.m." Well then, find five to fifteen minutes beforehand to do some deep work, and schedule the longer periods of deep work for just after that when you can. Morning is the best time for this.

If you need to get kids up and ready for the day, Admiral McRaven always said: *"Do something powerful in the morning. Make your bed."* Do the most important things first before you get sucked into someone else's agenda or the distractions of the day. Box breathe. Do twenty burpees. Meditate. Pray. Do something important and powerful for yourself. The great news is others around you will benefit.

Look at your life as one big practice . . . for life. If this sounds impossible because moments with your kids or significant other take you off track from your morning ritual, draw them into it. I tell the story in my second book, *Kokoro Yoga*, that when I would practice yoga, Devon, my then five-year-old son, would come lie on my back. Pretty soon, Devon became a regular, enjoying the up-dog, down-dog carnival ride on Dad daily. It became a different practice and required a different level of concentration on my part, but the playful, loving connection was worth it.

LAST ACTIONS, WORDS, AND THOUGHTS

In the evenings, start being mindful of your last actions and your last words to yourself or loved ones. This will become habitual like your morning mantra over time.

Once you are in bed, I know some of you like to wind down watching TV. Try to steer clear of social media and anything that'll rile up the senses. You want to shut down the engine. Reading can be a nice way to calm your brain waves. Then, consider some words of gratitude to your loved ones, followed by a silent prayer or mantra as your last internally crafted words. Then, just go to sleep.

If some thought pattern from unfinished business or a regret keeps coming up, preventing you from falling to sleep, take a minute to process it. Turn on the light, grab your journal, and write it down. Then spend a couple minutes contemplating it and let it go.

Then, lie down again and close your eyes, grateful to have made it to the end of your One Day.

I like to read for a while or play solitaire or practice a language with Duolingo to empty my mind of random thoughts. I will do some relaxation breathing as I consider my last words with my wife—usually the best things about the day. We take time to celebrate the "one day, one lifetime" we have together. Even when you experience a crisis, if you're still here, you can be grateful for something. Feed your courage wolf, regardless of your circumstances.

My final, final thoughts are always ones of gratitude and thanks to the Creator. Any unresolved questions or issues, I send out to the universe and ask for help and guidance. I ask for protection for myself, my loved ones, and my family. Then, I shut my brain down and surrender to sleep.

LET GO TO FLOW

In that big space between first thoughts and last thoughts, as you execute your daily challenges or tasks, you want to expand. Don't contract.

This is how you let go and connect to your witness.

- Let go of doing things for selfish reasons.
- Let go of doing things without realizing the interconnectedness and higher order of all things.
- Let go of expectations and attachment to results.
- Accept what is, all the time, relentlessly.

You'll find much more flow in your activities. You'll find greater peace of mind and enjoyment.

And you'll develop humility around the outcomes of your actions, which may lead to wealth and great notoriety, or you might remain an unsung hero. They're both okay. If you're acting from your higher power, expanding from your higher self, and focused on your mission, you are mastering your five mountains of consciousness.

Before moving on to the final exercise, let's check in on the gap to see how far you've come since starting your Uncommon Journey!

Remember: We measure your success from where you started to where you are now. We measure your progress.

1. You have made one or more lifestyle changes that have improved your eating habits and your physical stamina, strength, and flexibility.
2. You are thinking about your thinking when you first wake up. This is metacognition—the way to controlling your monkey mind.
3. You have created one or more positive morning mantras that you practice habitually.

4. You now have multiple concentration techniques at your disposal: box breathing, focusing on a candle flame, Zen counting practice, the body scan.

5. You are developing positive self-talk by interdicting fear with words of kindness. In this way, you are becoming a master of your emotions and emotional default states, and you are creating new, transformational loops in your neuroplastic brain. Focus and determination emanate from the courageous. That's you!

6. You're practicing contemplative journaling to uncover your likes, dislikes, your archetype, and your *why*.

7. You're practicing visualization, a whole body-mind drill to realize your dreams: *See it. Feel it. Believe it. Say it. Do it.* You are living this daily! Doubt is eliminated through action.

8. Through a process called *recapitulation*, you have worked on ridding your mind of emotional traumas from the past.

9. You are working daily at mastering inner and outer awareness to develop your transrational and inferential intuition to create holistic awareness. This will allow you to feel, think, speak, and act from a place of truth.

10. With the heart intuition as your guide, you are forging deeper connections with the people around you. This requires present-moment awareness, which leads to a more passionate life.

11. You are practicing the most effective sensory aware-

ness training to hone your intuition: mindfulness meditation. It connects your head to the insights your heart and gut are sending. The intuitive, perceiving mind is an open hand waiting to receive inspiration and intuitive signals from that future all-knowing Source—and you are now tuned in!

12. You are practicing first thoughts, last thoughts, and mindfulness all day long between those thoughts. You're on the journey to self-mastery.

When you feel stuck, sitting in meditation will always bring clarity to who you really are and how you can best serve humanity to create your Uncommon Life filled with purpose and joy.

Remember: We can't do life alone. We are all connected.

Can you believe how far you've come in such a short time? You have set yourself up for success. Congratulations!

What's that? You don't feel ready? You're not clear on your calling? *Your monkey mind still gets the best of you?*

That's the best news ever. That means you're thinking about your thinking. And if you're still carrying the girl from the river crossing, put her down already and get on with your day!

See it. Feel it. Believe it. Say it. Do it!

EXERCISE 15
Sacred Silence

Sacred silence is the art of learning to become comfortable while being alone and receptive to messages from the all-knowing voice or Source.

People have talked to me about being uncomfortable in the state of aloneness. I haven't brought it up yet because all these exercises require you to be alone (or at least silent), and I didn't want you to overthink it. However, the more you learn to still your thoughts and open your heart, the more you'll be able to tune in to the messages from your inner awareness, your surroundings, and the people around you. All this alone time—box breathing, concentration practices, mindfulness meditation, contemplative journaling—is to increase your present-moment awareness so you can communicate with yourself and others truthfully and intimately in any capacity you wish. This aloneness will make you a master of togetherness.

I first learned the power of going into nature alone as a teen. I would just be present. Let my brain meander. Let everything slow down. Even my thoughts would slow down. You get this resonance with the natural world when you're still and in nature. Time really does stop, and when that happens, you are free. Energetically, it's a great place (and a very effective way) to tap into and cultivate your spiritual intelligence.

Find a spot outside that's comfortable, where you feel safe and connected to Mother Earth. Journaling can be used to strengthen pattern recognition to increase self-awareness to better fulfill your mission, so have your journal handy.

Box breathe for five or more minutes to drop into your witness.

Then, begin a mindfulness meditation practice. Breathe deeply and imagine your consciousness dropping into the heart region and expanding it. Surrender to the experience. Pick an intention for this practice if you'd like. It's a good idea to ask the "all-knowing" for permission to ask a question. So, if something's on your mind, ask permission to ask about it . . . and then ask away. Make sure to free your mind to be open to whatever answers come your way.

After you become the mountain watching the thought clouds pass by, journal what comes up. Do this for the next five or more minutes. This will help you become more sensitive to what's going on in your inner mind and with your emotions.

Nice work.

1. So, what came up?
2. What patterns did you notice?
3. How do some of the thoughts you wrote down make you feel as you revisit them?

Over time, once you become comfortable with this practice, you can get even more specific, as I did when I studied with Nakamura.

Here are two ways how:

- If there's an issue, reach out to your inferential intuition in the form of a question, and then free your mind, preparing yourself for whatever sensation or answer arises.
- If you're interested in receiving transrational information, set a positive intention and feel into that as you free your mind and become the mountain.

BONUS EXERCISE 4
20X Sacred Silence!

Try being silent for twenty-four hours. (If you sleep for eight, that's only sixteen hours!) Going into nature for a bit to walk, hike, or meditate will help you get through this practice. You can write in your journal periodically if you so desire or wait until the exercise is over to jot down your thoughts and feelings. (This means no smartphones.)

Good luck!

Conclusion

WHAT ARE YOU REALLY IN CHARGE OF?

Y ou're probably not in charge of enforcing international law and maintaining peace and security worldwide. You're not likely in charge of the 5G towers that service over five hundred million people (as of 2021) with greater bandwidth and faster cell phone connections. You're not in charge of temperature control on Mars or mapping the thousand-mile-plus migration paths of leatherback turtles. And you're not in charge of what I'm going to wear to work next Tuesday. Sandy is. *JK.*

But, as Stephen Covey of *The 7 Habits of Highly Effective People* says, you are in charge of *"those things in your sphere of influence."*

You're in control of your internal evolution. You have an imperative to grow, to be the best version of yourself possible. You're responsible for that growth, especially as you move into adulthood. Nobody else can do this for you. You're responsible for choosing the food and forms of exercise that nourish and strengthen your system.

You're in charge of controlling your thoughts and emotions and directing them toward positive action in alignment with your mission. Your thoughts and emotions must serve you. If they aren't, they're holding you back.

You're in charge of determining what your mission is, developing a powerful vision for your future, and executing it. You're in charge of that. No one can tell you what that is or do it for you.

Since we don't go through life alone, because we have teams and relationships to manage, you're in charge of the quality of your relationships with your family, friends, and teams. You may think you're being affected by others, but your words, thoughts, and actions are your responsibility. Clear communication—this includes mastering both talking and listening skills—is on you. Take responsibility for that. The Apostle Paul says, "As much as depends on you, be at peace with all men."

You're responsible for how you show up every day. What do you put your focus on?

You're responsible for 100 percent of your hair-on-fire warrior commitment, for the quality of your attitude, your drive, and for maintaining humility in everything you do.

You're responsible for unlocking your creative intuition. No one can do it for you. You've got to do the work: Check in with your heart. Trust your gut. Learn the language. Practice using the tool. Master the skills. Strengthen your *kokoro*.

Stop grasping for answers and surrender to presence. Let wisdom flow through you.

You're 100 percent responsible for your successes and your failures. It's no one else's fault but yours if a project flops or a relationship goes south.[1]

You're responsible for your attitude toward success or failure. Appreciate the success without becoming attached to it, and give thanks for your support system and other people's contributions. Take 100 percent responsibility when failure comes. This is how spiritual intelligence works. Act on what you've learned from your setbacks. Doubt is eliminated through action. When you master your other four intelligences, spirituality wraps all your hard work in faith. Trust the process and trust your path!

With the notion of being 100 percent in charge, you stop blaming others. You stop being a victim. You stop expecting time, money, compliments, sacrifices, or other handouts from anyone. Matthew Engelhart, founder of Café Gratitude, says: *"Expectations suck the joy out of life."* Stop presuming others can read your mind or should carry you in any way. Stop holding them to a list of rules in your head. This creates conditions and restrictions—*sucks the joy from life*—and you are now free. You're living your life in alignment with your vision, and no one can change that.

This book is the way or "path" that my team and tribe at Unbeatable adhere to daily. It's a path because there is no destination, as it is continuously unfolding. For years now, I have experienced how awesome it is to live these principles, and I want you to experience that also. It's deeply inspiring.

It's a meditation in itself. Every day, I ask myself: *What can I let go of to spark more magic? How can I focus on the creative work of writing, podcasting, and speaking more effectively? How committed can I be to my "one day, one life" practice of first and last words, of thoughts, of actions? How can I develop more clarity for my future and for everyone my company connects with through that process?*

Over the last decade, this lifestyle has built up an enormous amount of momentum. These principles allow me to live with passion. I'm able to refine, realign, and fine-tune my vision more efficiently with every new sunrise I'm blessed to experience. My teams are inspired by that. We support each other, because we're on the mission together. This catalyzes growth for all involved, this sense of connection.

Since the mid-twentieth century, theoretical and quantum physicists have been on the hunt for the equation that expresses the theory of everything (ToE)—a common field that connects the stars in the sky to the snailfish deep in the ocean to the devil worm tunneling miles under the earth's surface. This is a fundamental truth to most indigenous peoples of the world. *"The Sioux say mitakuye oyasin, which means 'all is related.' . . . From the Aborigines in Australia to the Dogon tribes of Africa to the Maori tribes of New Zealand, these indigenous people all believe everything we can and cannot see shares a common connection."*[2]

You will likely never be able to quantify the effects of your thoughts and actions on the world. You'd have to track the lifespan of a thought put into action and measure its effect on everything to do that. And we don't have that capacity, at least not today. But it's not unreasonable to assume the positive ones will have a more positive effect than the negative ones. And all thoughts put into action affect you—and go beyond your sphere of influence—as we are all connected. This is why I devoted so much time to the importance of mastering whole mind thinking, where our thoughts originate.

You were meant to be extraordinary, and now you're ready. Using your **Uncommon Vision,** you can now tap into your personal power and find your purpose. With your **Uncommon Tools,** you can harness your 20X potential. Charged with **Uncommon Mental Toughness,** you can root yourself in your **Uncommon Stand** to manage life's challenges while your **Uncommon Beliefs** charge your passion daily. Your time to be Uncommon is now.

You're a train that has left the station, a rocket ship that's been launched. We are all built with limitless potential. And we've just unleashed yours.

You have begun your journey to an Uncommon Life.

Now go grab hold of your destiny.

WHO DID INVENT THE WHEEL?

The wheel is considered by many to be the greatest invention of all time. Based on archaeological evidence, Mesopotamian cultures are believed to have been the original inventors. These first wheels, appearing between the Neolithic and Bronze Ages, were used for making pottery. It would be two thousand years or so before the ancient Greeks attached wheels to an axle (creating carts), which they used to transport materials for building structures such as the Parthenon.

The reason the wheel has been revered as the zenith of all inventions is because wheels don't exist in nature. You can find forked sticks, levers, swings, pitchforks but nothing that mirrors a cylinder with a hole in the center with which to insert a rod. This took some deep focus over the course of tens of thousands of years to conceive. And it was only through a series of well-thought-out steps that early man went from studying a cylindrical object in all its potential to attaching a functioning, rotating axle between two of these "donut-type thingies" and reducing friction to the point where the contraption could rotate.[3]

The invention of the wheel gave us wheelbarrows, bicycles, chariots, mills, tools, gears, more sophisticated vehicles of transportation, and the list goes on. The wheel, some say, single-handedly created civilization as we know it.

Without even being conscious of it, we refer to the invention of the wheel in our everyday vernacular. *"I don't want to be a fifth wheel." "We're not trying to reinvent the wheel here." "The wheels have really come off this deal."* And my personal favorite: *"This guy thinks he invented the wheel."*

Who knows? If you believe in reincarnation, maybe I did invent the wheel.

Or maybe you did. Think about that as you move forward on your **Uncommon Path**.

From my kokoro spirit to yours, thank you for your time. We've got this . . . easy day!

—**Mark Divine**

ACKNOWLEDGMENTS

Thanks to all my teachers, mentors, coaches, teammates, and followers on the path to being uncommon. I appreciate you all very much . . . and am excited to continue the work and the mission. One hundred million.

NOTES

INTRODUCTION

1. "Common Definition & Meaning," *Merriam-Webster,* accessed May 16, 2023, www.merriam-webster.com/dictionary/common.

2. Katie Serena, "She Has the Highest I.Q. Ever Recorded—and Her Name Is Actually 'Savant,'" All That's Interesting, September 4, 2022, https://allthatsinteresting.com/marilyn-vos-savant.

3. "Men's 100m Olympic Final | This Is Who Is Now Dubbed the 'World's Fastest Man,'" 11Alive, 2021, https://www.11alive.com/article/sports/olympics/mens-100m-olympic-final-who-will-be-worlds-fastest-man/85-f3ffa1ce-8170-4b19-b1fd-e62a915374e2.

4. "Newton's Laws | Boundless Physics," Course Hero, accessed May 16, 2023, https://courses.lumenlearning.com/boundless-physics/chapter/newtons-laws/.

5. Jim Taylor, "Four Forces of Life Inertia," *Psychology Today,* December 5, 2011, https://www.psychologytoday.com/us/blog/the-power-prime/201112/four-forces-life-inertia.

6. Andrew Zimmerman Jones, "Inertia and the Laws of Motion." Thought Co, updated on August 11, 2019, https://www.thoughtco.com/inertia-2698982.

1: THE POWER OF MOMENTUM

1. Natalie O'Neill, "Scientist May Have Figured Out Why Women Live Longer than Men," *New York Post,* March 4, 2020, https://nypost.com/2020/03/04/scientist-may-have-figured-out-why-women-live-longer-than-men/.

2. Goodarz Danaei, Eric L. Ding, Dariush Mozaffarian, Ben Taylor, Jürgen Rehm, Christopher J. L. Murray, and Majid Ezzati, "The Preventable Causes of Death in the United States: Comparative Risk Assessment of Dietary, Lifestyle, and Metabolic Risk Factors," *PLOS Medicine* 6, no. 4 (April 28, 2009): e1000058, https://doi.org/10.1371/journal.pmed.1000058.

3. Diego Silva, Augusto Santos, Mark S. Tremblay, Fatima Marinho, Antonio Luiz Pinho Ribeiro, Ewerton Cousin, Bruno Ramos Nascimento, Paulo da Fonseca Valença Neto, Mohsen Naghavi, and Deborah Carvalho Malta, "Physical Inactivity as a Risk Factor for All-Cause Mortality in Brazil (1990–2017)," *Population Health Metrics* 18, no. S1 (September 30, 2020): https://doi.org/10.1186/s12963-020-00214-3.

4. Goldfine, Rebecca, "Olympian Joan Benoit Samuelson '79 Reflects on Championship, Mental Health, and Balance," *Bowdoin* (August 03, 2021): https://www.bowdoin.edu/news/2021/08/olympian-joan-benoit-samuelson-79-reflects-on-championship-mental-health-and-priorities.html.

2: MOVE THE BODY, GROW THE MIND

1. Mark P. Mattson, "Evolutionary Aspects of Human Exercise—Born to Run Purposefully," *Ageing Research Reviews* 11, no. 3 (July 1, 2012): 347–52, https://doi.org/10.1016/j.arr.2012.01.007.

2. Marion Webb, "Increase Energy Levels and Cure Fatigue Through Exercise," Ace Fitness, September 8, 2011, https://www.bowdoin.edu/news/2021/08/olympian-joan-benoit-samuelson-79-reflects-on-championship-mental-health-and-priorities.

3. Alexa Tucker and Christa Sgobba, C.P/T., "10 Amazing Benefits of Exercise That Are Extra Important to Hear Right Now," *SELF,* April 1, 2020, https://www.self.com/story/11-amazing-reasons-to-work-out-that-have-nothing-to-do-with-weight-loss.

4. Melinda Smith, M.A., Lawrence Robinson, and Jeanne Segal, Ph.D., "Post-Traumatic Stress Disorder (PTSD)," HelpGuide.Org, last updated or reviewed on March 27, 2023, https://www.helpguide.org/articles/ptsd-trauma/ptsd-symptoms-self-help-treatment.htm.

5. Tucker and Sgobba.

6. Mattson.

7. Melinda Smith, M.A., Jeanne Segal, Ph.D., and Lawrence Robinson, "How to Improve Your Memory," HelpGuide.Org, last updated or reviewed on June 28, 2023. https://www.helpguide.org/articles/healthy-living/how-to-improve-your-memory.htm.

8. David Hawkins, *The Ultimate David Hawkins Library*, https://www.audible.com/pd/The-Ultimate-David-Hawkins-Library-Audiobook/B01ENWKFOQ.

9. Amogh, "How to Effortlessly Lose Weight *For Real*, According to Dr David R Hawkins," *The Examined Life*, January 10, 2021, https://examinedlife.substack.com/p/weight-loss.

10. Tricia Christensen, "What Is the Appestat?" TheHealthBoard, last modified on April 18, 2023, https://www.thehealthboard.com/what-is-the-appestat.htm.

11. Gabrielle Mancella, RD, "How Too Much Stress Can Cause Weight Gain (and What to Do about It)," Orlando Health, February 12, 2020, https://www.orlandohealth.com/content-hub/how-too-much-stress-can-cause-weight-gain-and-what-to-do-about-it.

12. W. Jean Dodds, DVM, "How Your Pet's Brain and Body Regulate His Appetite," *Animal Wellness Magazine,* November 28, 2018, https://animalwellnessmagazine.com/pets-brain-body-regulate-appetite/.

13. Martin P. Wegman, Michael H. Guo, Douglas M. Bennion, Meena N. Shankar, Stephen M. Chrzanowski, Leslie A. Goldberg, Jinze Xu, Tiffany A. Williams, Xiaomin Lu, Stephen I. Hsu, Stephen D. Anton, Christiaan Leeuwenburgh, and Mark L. Brantly, "Practicality of Intermittent Fasting in Humans and Its Effect on Oxidative Stress and Genes Related to Aging and Metabolism," *Rejuvenation Research* 18, no. 2 (April 1, 2015): 162–72, https://doi.org/10.1089/rej.2014.1624.

3: TEAMWORK MAKES THE DREAM WORK

1. "Jerry Rice," Pro Football Hall of Fame, accessed May 16, 2023, https://www.profootballhof.com/players/jerry-rice/.

2. "Jerry Rice's Football Success & Chiropractic," McMichael Chiropractor Natural Health & Wellness Clinic, accessed May 16, 2023, http://www.mcmichaelchiro.com/jerry-rices-football-success--chiropractic.html.

3. Bobby Warshaw, "Pro Athletes Have a Lot of People to Thank for Success. Here's Bobby Warshaw's List," *PennLive*, June 18, 2013, https://www.pennlive.com/sports/2013/06/pro_athletes_thanks_bobby_warshaw.html.

4. Olly Roberts, "Belinda Bencic, Marketa Vondrousova: Who Are the Tokyo Olympics Women's Tennis Finalists?" *GiveMeSport*, July 29, 2021, https://www.givemesport.com/1730018-belinda-bencic-marketa-vondrousova-who-are-the-tokyo-olympics-womens-tennis-finalists.

5. "George Shinn," Horatio Alger Association of Distinguished Americans, Inc., accessed May 16, 2023, https://horatioalger.org/members/member-detail/george-shinn.

6. National Academies of Sciences, Engineering, and Medicine; Division of Behavioral and Social Sciences and Education; Health and Medicine Division; Board on Behavioral, Cognitive, and Sensory Sciences; Board on Health Sciences Policy; Committee on the Health and Medical Dimensions of Social Isolation and Loneliness in Older Adults, "Social Isolation and Loneliness in Older Adults: Opportunities for the Health Care System," NCBI Bookshelf, February 27, 2020, https://www.ncbi.nlm.nih.gov/books/NBK557977/.

7. Emma Seppälä, "Connectedness & Health: The Science of Social Connection," The Center for Compassion and Altruism Research and Education, May 8, 2014, http://ccare.stanford.edu/uncategorized/connectedness-health-the-science-of-social-connection-infographic/.

8. Emma Seppälä, "Social Connection Boosts Health, Even When You're Isolated," *Psychology Today*, March 23, 2020, https://www.psychologytoday.com/us/blog/feeling-it/202003/social-connection-boosts-health-even-when-youre-isolated.

9. Simon Bell, "Human Nature: Not as Bad as We Think We Are," MindTools, February 10, 2022, https://www.mindtools.com/blog/human-nature-not-as-bad-as-we-think-we-are/.

10. Andrea J. Becker, "It's Not What They Do, It's How They Do It: Athlete Experiences of Great Coaching," *International Journal of Sports Science & Coaching* 4, no. 1 (March 1, 2009): 93–119, https://doi.org/10.1260/1747-9541.4.1.93.

4: HARNESSING YOUR 20X MIND POWER

1. "How Meditation Raises Your Vibration, Positive Energy," EOC Institute, accessed May 16, 2023, https://eocinstitute.org/meditation/meditation-and-energy-raising-your-vibrations-for-a-fulfilling-life/.

2. Christine Comaford, "Got Inner Peace? 5 Ways To Get It NOW," *Forbes*, April 4, 2012, https://www.forbes.com/sites/christinecomaford/2012/04/04/got-inner-peace-5-ways-to-get-it-now/?sh=13c361926672.

3. Charmaine Husum, DKATI, RTC, CT, "Default Mode Network: Ego vs. Mindfulness," Linden & Arc Vitality Institute, accessed May 16, 2023, https://lynnemurfinmd.com/blog-posts/what-is-your-default-mode -network/.

4. Maria Popova, "Fixed vs. Growth: The Two Basic Mindsets That Shape Our Lives," *The Marginalian*, accessed May 16, 2023, https://www .brainpickings.org/2014/01/29/carol-dweck-mindset/.

5. Dweck, Carol S. 2006. *Mindset: The New Psychology of Success*. New York: Ballantine Books.

5: YOUR FUTURE IS NOW

1. Jason Kottke, "The Story of Two Monks and a Woman," *Kottke.org*, January 26, 2020, https://kottke.org/20/01/the-story-of-two-monks-and-a -woman.

2. Jay W. Marks, MD, "Medical Definition of Neuroplasticity," MedicineNet, reviewed on June 3, 2021, https://www.medicinenet.com/neuroplasticity /definition.htm.

3. "Sahaja Yoga Meditation Increases Gray Matter in the Brain, Study Finds," *PsyPost*, September 11, 2016, https://www.psypost.org/2016/09/sahaja-yoga -meditation-increases-gray-matter-brain-study-finds-44886.

4. "Svadharma," Encyclopedia.com, accessed May 16, 2023, https://www .encyclopedia.com/religion/dictionaries-thesauruses-pictures-and-press -releases/svadharma.

5. Conor Neill, "Understanding Personality: The 12 Jungian Archetypes" *Moving People to Action*, April 21, 2018, https://conorneill.com/2018/04 /21/understanding-personality-the-12-jungian-archetypes/.

6. "Vikramjit Singh (Comedian) Height, Weight, Age, Wife, Biography & More," StarsUnfolded, accessed May 16, 2023, https://starsunfolded.com /vikramjit-singh/.

6: ENVISION YOUR DESTINY

1. Caroline Delbert, "Elon Musk: Mars Isn't for Rich People—It's for Explorers Who Will 'Probably Die,'" *Popular Mechanics*, April 26, 2021, https://www.popularmechanics.com/space/moon-mars/a36230702/elon -musk-mars-settlers-will-probably-die/.

2. Nancy Newell, "The Hidden Power of Visualization," *Nancynewell.com*, February 6, 2019.

3. Catherine Plano, "From Imagination to Reality: Using Visualization for Success," Ellevate, accessed May 16, 2023, https://www.ellevatenetwork.com/articles/7650-from-imagination-to-reality-using-visualization-for-success.

4. Petros Eshetu, "The 6 Best Brian Tracy Books (to Read in 2023)," *UpJourney,* December 14, 2022, https://upjourney.com/best-brian-tracy-books.

7: THE POWER OF EMOTIONS

1. "Emotion," *Stanford Encyclopedia of Philosophy,* first published on September 25, 2018, https://plato.stanford.edu/entries/emotion/.

8: FEED COURAGE

1. Bill Fields, "Lee Elder, a Trailblazer and Four-Time TOUR Winner, Passes Away at 87," PGA Tour, accessed May 16, 2023, https://www.pgatour.com/news/2021/11/29/lee-elder-passes-away-age-87-pga-tour.html.

2. Fit4D, "The Neuroscience of Behavior Change," *Medium,* August 8, 2017, https://healthtransformer.co/the-neuroscience-of-behavior-change-bcb567fa83c1.

9: REWRITE YOUR STORY

1. "About Gary Kraftsow," American Viniyoga Institute, accessed May 16, 2023, https://viniyoga.com/about/gary-kraftsow/.

2. Dr. Candace Pert, "Physics of Emotion: Candace Pert on Feeling Good," interview by Joshua Freedman, Six Seconds: The Emotional Intelligence Network, accessed May 16, 2023, https://www.6seconds.org/2007/01/26/the-physics-of-emotion-candace-pert-on-feeling-good/.

3. Peter Fisk, "Time to Activate Your Happy Chemicals . . . Dopamine, Serotonin, Endorphins and Oxytocin." *Peter Fisk,* October 19, 2018. https://www.peterfisk.com/2018/10/time-to-activate-your-happy-chemicals-dopamine-serotonin-endorphins-and-oxytocin/.

4. "What Is BodyMind and How Can It Improve Your Health?" Rendezvous, accessed on May 16, 2023, https://www.rendezvouscolorado.com/wellness/blog/what-is-bodymind-and-how-can-it-improve-your-health/.

10: NO REGRETS

1. "Erno Rubik," Encyclopedia Britannica, accessed May 16, 2023, https://www.britannica.com/biography/Erno-Rubik.

2. "A Brief History of Emotional Intelligence," Practical Emotional Intelligence, accessed May 16, 2023, https://www.emotionalintelligencecourse.com/history-of-eq/.

11: THE POWER OF INTUITION

1. Frederick W. Smith, "I Don't Know, Probably Made My Usual C," Quote Investigator, December 12, 2017, https://quoteinvestigator.com/2017/12/12/fedex/.

2. Brian Resnick, "What America Looked Like: The 1970s Gas Crisis," *The Atlantic,* May 31, 2012, https://www.theatlantic.com/national/archive/2012/05/what-america-looked-like-the-1970s-gas-crisis/257837/.

3. Ann Schmidt, "How Fred Smith Rescued FedEx from Bankruptcy by Playing Blackjack in Las Vegas," *Fox Business,* July 19, 2020, https://www.foxbusiness.com/money/fred-smith-fedex-blackjack-winning-formula.

4. Marrecca Flore, "Study Finds Empathy Can Be Detected in People Whose Brains Are at Rest," UCLA Newsroom, February 18, 2020, https://newsroom.ucla.edu/releases/empathy-detected-brains-at-rest.

5. Matthew A. J. Apps, Patricia L. Lockwood, and Joshua H. Balsters, "The Role of the Midcingulate Cortex in Monitoring Others' Decisions," *Frontiers in Neuroscience* 7 (December 20, 2013): https://doi.org/10.3389/fnins.2013.00251.

6. Courtney Helgoe, "5 Gut Instincts You Shouldn't Ignore," Experience Life By Life Time, November 1, 2020, https://experiencelife.lifetime.life/article/5-gut-instincts-you-shouldnt-ignore/#top.

7. Pilar Gerasimo and Dallas Hartwig, "The Living Experiment: Intuition," *Experience Life By Life Time,* September 10, 2018, https://experiencelife.lifetime.life/article/the-living-experiment-intuition/.

12: THE SECOND BRAIN

1. "The Brain-Gut Connection," Johns Hopkins Medicine, accessed May 16, 2023, https://www.hopkinsmedicine.org/health/wellness-and-prevention/the-brain-gut-connection.

2. John B. Furness, "The Enteric Nervous System and Neurogastroenterology," *Nature Reviews: Gastroenterology & Hepatology* 9, no. 5 (May 1, 2012): 286–94, https://doi.org/10.1038/nrgastro.2012.32.

3. Carly Vandergriendt, "What's the Difference Between Dopamine and Serotonin?," medically reviewed by Femi Aremu, PharmD, *Healthline,*

July 16, 2020, https://www.healthline.com/health/dopamine-vs-serotonin #depression.

4. Tom Brown, Jr., "Concentric Rings," Wildwood Tracking, 1984, https:// www.wildwoodtracking.com/awareness/trm/trm3-1pg04.html.

5. "Where Are Memories Stored in the Brain?," Queensland Brain Institute, accessed May 16, 2023, https://qbi.uq.edu.au/brain-basics/memory /where-are-memories-stored.

13: HEART INTUITION

1. Rollin McCraty, PhD, Mike Atkinson, Raymond Threvor Bradley, PhD, "Electrophysiological Evidence of Intuition: Part 1. The Surprising Role of the Heart," *The Journal of Alternative and Complementary Medicine* 10, no. 1 (November 1, 2004): 133–43, https://www.heartmath.org/assets /uploads/2015/01/intuition-part1.pdf.

2. Femke S. Ten Velden, Katie Daughters, and Carsten K. W. De Dreu, "Oxytocin Promotes Intuitive Rather than Deliberated Cooperation with the In-Group," *Hormones and Behavior* 92 (June 1, 2017): 164–71, https:// doi.org/10.1016/j.yhbeh.2016.06.005.

3. Pilar Gerasimo and Dallas Hartwig.

4. Jill Thomas, "Intuition vs Paranoia & How to Tell the Difference Between the Two," Soul Connect Transformations, October 1, 2019, https://www .jillkthomas.com/blog/intuition-vs-paranoia/.

5. Raymond Trevor Bradley, "The Psychophysiology of Entrepreneurial Intuition: A Quantum-Holographic Theory," *Proceedings of the Third AGSE International Entrepreneurship Research Exchange*, February 8–10, 2006, https://www.heartmath.org/assets/uploads/2015/01/bradley -psychophysiology-of-entreprenuerial-intuition.

14: LIVE LIFE VIRTUOUSLY

1. Ephrat Livni, "This Japanese Word Connecting Mind, Body, and Spirit Is Also Driving Scientific Discovery," *Quartz*, April 6, 2017, https://qz.com /946438/kokoro-a-japanese-word-connecting-mind-body-and-spirit-is -also-driving-scientific-discovery/.

15: ONE DAY, ONE LIFE

1. Liz Masen, "Coaching: Get the Initial 15% Right, and the Remaining 85% Will Follow," LinkedIn, August 25, 2014, https://www.linkedin.com

/pulse/20140825231947–34445325-coaching-get-the-initial-15-right-and
-the-remaining-85-will-follow/.

2. Newport, Cal. Deep Work: Rules for Focused Success in a Distracted
    World. New York: Grand Central Publishing, 2016.

CONCLUSION: WHAT ARE YOU REALLY IN CHARGE OF?

1. "What is Extreme Ownership?" Echelon Front, accessed May 16, 2023,
    https://echelonfront.com/extreme-ownership/.

2. Laurie Brenner, "What Is the Theory of Everything Scientists Talk About?,"
    Sciencing, updated on March 29, 2018, https://sciencing.com/what-is-the
    -theory-of-everything-scientists-talk-about-13710339.html.

3. Robert Krulwich, "Why'd It Take So Long To Invent the Wheel?," NPR,
    September 16, 2011, https://www.npr.org/sections/krulwich/2011/09/15
    /140508448/whyd-it-take-so-long-to-invent-the-wheel.

ABOUT THE AUTHOR

MARK DIVINE is a former Navy SEAL and has trained thousands of special operations candidates and operators. He owns and runs the SEALFIT Training Center in San Diego, California, where he trains thousands of professional athletes, military professionals, SWAT, first responders, SOF candidates, and everyday people looking to build strength and character.

With a background shaped by early immersion in Eastern philosophy and Zen meditation during his tenure at Price-Waterhouse Coopers, Mark's life took a decisive turn at twenty-six, when he emerged as the honor-man of his SEAL BUD/S class. His distinguished military career spanned two decades, culminating in his retirement as a commander. Beyond the battlefield, his leadership left an indelible mark through a nationwide mentoring program for SEAL trainees, significantly shaping the future of Navy SEALs.

As an author, Mark has penned numerous bestsellers, including *Unbeatable Mind, 8 Weeks to SEALFIT, The Way of the SEAL,* and *Staring Down the Wolf.* His books have been cited for their profound insights into peak performance and mental resilience. And as the host of *The Mark Divine Show,* a top-rated podcast in its ninth season with over five thousand five-star reviews and having reached over thirty million downloads, Mark engages with thought leaders and visionaries from various fields. Mark's ability to distill complex ideas into actionable wisdom has not only earned the podcast thousands of loyal listeners but has also positioned it as a crucial platform for those seeking growth and transformation in their personal and professional lives.

Beyond business success, Mark channels his energies into philanthropy and scholarship. The Mark Divine Courage Foundation, founded to aid veterans with PTSD, leads the global "Burpees for Vets Challenge," which annually raises over $500 mllion for veterans. Mark has a Ph.D. in Global Leadership and Change from Pepperdine University, where he continues to blend real-world experience with academic rigor.

A family man, Mark values his roles as a husband, father, and grandfather above all. Residing in Encinitas, California, Mark's life is a testament to the relentless pursuit of self-improvement, service, and the courage to embrace the unknown, inspiring others to transform and reach beyond their limits.